# What Ivan Knows That Johnny Doesn't

# What Ivan Knows That Johnny Doesn't

ARTHER S. TRACE, JR.

Random House : New York

FIRST PRINTING

© Copyright, 1961, by Arther S. Trace, Jr.
All rights reserved under International and Pan-American Copyright
Conventions. Published in New York by Random House, Inc., and
simultaneously in Toronto, Canada, by Random House of Canada, Limited.
Library of Congress Catalog Card Number: 61–14894
Manufactured in the United States of America by H. Wolff, New York

# ACKNOWLEDGMENTS

The author wishes to thank the following for permission to reprint material included in this book:

American Book Company—for selection on pages 31 and 33, from *Open Windows,* the first-grade volume of the Golden Rule Series in The Modern McGuffey Readers, by Ullin W. Leavell, Mary Louise Frieble, Tracie Cushman, and Alex M. Caughran.

Bobbs-Merrill Company, Inc.—for selection on page 21, from *Our Happy Ways,* by William H. Burton, Clara Belle Baker, and Grace K. Kemp, Copyright © 1950, 1959.

Follett Publishing Company—for selection on pages 161-162, from *Friends Near and Far,* by J. G. Meyer, Frank E. Sorenson, and Alta McIntire, Copyright 1949;—for selection pages 164-166, from *Exploring the Old World,* by Stuart Hamer, Orlando W. Stephenson, Ralph Sandlin Yohe, Ben F. Ahlschwede, Dwight W. Follett, and Herbert H. Gross, Copyright © 1955, 1957.

Ginn and Company—for selection on pages 43 and 45, from *This Is Our Valley,* the third-grade reader in the Faith and Freedom Series, by Sister Mary Marguerite and others;—for selection on pages 91, 93, and 95, from *Doorways to Discovery,* the seventh-grade reader in the Ginn Basic Readers series, by David H. Russell, Mabel Snedaker, and Doris Gates.

Harcourt, Brace & World, Inc.—for selection on pages 97, 99, and 101, from the Olympic Edition of Adventures for Readers, edited by Egbert W. Nieman and Elizabeth C. O'Daly;—for selection on pages 103 and 105, from the Olympic Edition of Adventures in Reading, edited by Evan Lodge and Marjorie Braymer;—for selection on pages 109 and 111, from the Mercury Edition of Adventures in Appreciation, edited by Luella B. Cook, Walter Loban, and Susanna Baxter.

Holt, Rinehart and Winston, Inc.—for selection on pages 37 and 39, from *People on Parade,* by Russell G. Stauffer, Alvina T. Burrows, and Evelyn R. Spencer, The John C. Winston Company, a division of Holt, Rinehart and Winston, Inc., © 1960;—for selection on page 137, from *Story of Nations,* by Rogers, Adams, and Brown, © 1960.

Houghton Mifflin Company—for selection on pages 85, 87 and 89, from *Bright Peaks,* the sixth-grade reader in the Reading for Meaning series, by Paul McKee, Annie McCowen, M. L. Harrison, and Elizabeth Lehr, Copyright © 1957.

The Macmillan Company—for selection on page 28, from *The World I Know* (Teacher's Manual), the fifth-grade book in The Macmillan Readers series, by Arthur I. Gates and Celeste Comegys Peardon, Copyright 1951;—for selection on pages 79 and 81, from *A World to Enjoy,* the fifth-grade reader in The Macmillan Readers series, by Arthur I. Gates and Celeste Comegys Peardon, Copyright 1953;—for selection on page 139, from *Living Together in the Old World,* the sixth-grade book in The Macmillan Social Studies series, by Prudence Cutright, Walter Lefferts, Harry H. Shapiro, and Israel Soifer, © 1958.

# Acknowledgments

Row, Peterson and Company—for selection on pages 21-22, from *Day In and Day Out*, the basic primer of The Alice and Jerry Basic Reading Program, by Mabel O'Donnell and others;—for selection on page 49, from *Singing Wheels*, the fourth-grade reader in The Alice and Jerry Basic Reading Program, by Mabel O'Donnell and others.

# Contents

# What Ivan Knows That Johnny Doesn't

# INTRODUCTION

The challenge of Soviet technology in recent years has prompted many comparisons between the American and Soviet school systems. These studies originate from the growing realization that intellectual strength is one of the chief means by which the free world will check and defeat communism or by which communism will check and defeat the free world.

The concern of most of the recent comparative studies of American and Soviet schools has been to show that American schools are lagging woefully behind Soviet schools in the teaching of mathematics and the sciences. These studies have emphasized that whereas *all* Russian students who graduate from high school[*] have studied physics for five years, chemistry for four years, biology for six years, and astronomy for one year, only some American high school graduates have studied biology or physics or chemistry for one year. Hardly any have studied one of these subjects for more than a year, and very few have studied all three. Similarly, in the teaching of mathematics, American schools regularly lag two years behind Soviet

[*] See Appendix B.

3

schools, and a close look at the mathematics program of both school systems will show that in some places the lag is nearer three or even four years.

In view of the tremendous importance of education in the struggle between communism and the free world, this vast disparity between Soviet and American schools in the teaching of mathematics and the basic sciences is more than a little terrifying. Educators and school administrators readily admit, as they must, that this great disparity exists. Some efforts have been made to strengthen the science and mathematics programs, but the results thus far are inconclusive.

But American educators and laymen alike tend to take considerable comfort in the belief that in the American schools at least the other basic subjects, the subjects commonly referred to as the humanities—chiefly, literature and history—and the subjects closely related to the humanities, are in a thriving condition, whereas in the Soviet Union, so they think, the humanities run counter to Communist interests and are therefore suppressed in the Soviet schools. This book proposes to present some evidence which it is hoped will pretty thoroughly shatter that illusion. It proposes to show that the American system of education, especially at the elementary and the junior high school levels, is so far from being a bastion of the humanities that the humanities are, in fact, shamefully and dangerously neglected. Furthermore, it proposes to show that Soviet education, even though it uses the humanities and the subjects directly related to the humanities for the indoctrination of communism, affords its students vastly more thorough training in these subjects than American schools afford our students.

It is, of course, easier to generalize about Soviet schools than about American schools, because Soviet education is centralized, and the curriculum, textbooks, and standards are—with few exceptions—uniform throughout the Soviet Union; whereas in our country there is considerable variation in these respects

4

from state to state and from community to community. None-theless, it is possible to draw sound and important conclusions about our school system as a whole by examining the textbooks and the courses of study available to our students. I have not been concerned with American private schools in this study, however, because they educate only a small percentage of our students and the course of study in them is usually quite differ-ent from that of the other schools.

Anyone who wishes to determine the quality of the school system of his own community, state, or country, or the school system of any other country, may proceed in any of several ways. He may take a tour of a school or of a number of schools, examining the lighting and seating arrangements of the class-rooms, the audio-visual aid equipment, the library facilities, the gymnasium, and the hot-lunch program; or he may talk with teachers and school administrators and collect statistics about the number of students in the school, the size of the classes, the financial condition of the school system, and the qualifications of the teachers and the school administrators themselves. Or, lacking the opportunity to get this information first-hand, he may be content to form his impressions by reading written accounts by those who have made such tours.

All this information will, of course, contribute something to an understanding of how good or how bad a school system may be. But such information can be misleading, not only because it tends to be highly impressionistic but also because the school with the newest building, the most spacious library, the most modern gymnasium, the brightest classroom, the smallest classes, the shiniest equipment, and the hottest lunch program may still be a school in which very little learning is going on. There is, in fact, a strong tendency in this country to measure the quality of a school by examining the *conditions* under which children learn rather than examining *what* they learn.

The fact is that none of this information can provide more

than a fraction of what is needed to arrive at an accurate estimate of the quality of education which a school provides. By far the most important information to help determine the quality of education of any school or any school system is information about its curriculum and its textbooks. The curriculum reveals what subjects are studied, by whom, and for how long, but a study of the curriculum alone can also be misleading, particularly regarding American schools. For as this book will indicate, even though the curriculum at any given grade level may call for literature or reading or history, the amount of literature, reading, or history that is actually taught may often be slight indeed.

Wherever the curriculum is found to be satisfactory, there still remains the vital problem of the quality of the textbooks, for no one dares to underestimate the importance of textbooks in the teaching of any of the basic subjects. In fact, in such basic subjects as reading, literature, history, geography, and mathematics, textbooks are perhaps the heart of the school system, since even the best teacher is limited by the quality of the texts. Audio-visual aids, class discussions, visiting lecturers, and the teacher's own imparted knowledge and wisdom all contribute in varying degrees to our children's education in these basic subjects, but nothing contributes so much as their textbooks, for it is primarily textbooks which determine the organization and presentation of the material and the thoroughness with which the basic subjects are studied. Furthermore, students discuss textbook material in class, they are asked questions about it, they take tests on it, their homework assignments are usually based on it, and whatever else they do, they are expected to master it.

A textbook is in fact a tyrant, because the teacher is fairly well obliged to plan course work around it, particularly in teaching the basic subjects. And since in the future even the most ingenious teaching machines cannot be expected to replace textbooks in the basic subjects, it is more than likely that

6

the schools of the future, if they are to be good schools, will still have to rely heavily upon textbooks at all educational levels.

It will be evident, therefore, that if a student's textbooks are excellent he may be able to get an excellent education indeed if he has good teachers and if he studies hard; but if his textbooks are poor, his education is bound to be correspondingly poor no matter how excellent his teacher may be or how hard he studies. It matters even less whether his school building has the latest design, whether his classroom is spacious and well-lighted, or whether his gymnasium is fully equipped.

In the following chapters I shall make some comparisons between Soviet and American elementary and high school education in the areas of (1) reading, (2) literature, (3) foreign languages, (4) history, and (5) geography; and I shall base these comparisons upon an examination of the textbooks used in both school systems and upon an examination of the curricula.

These comparisons and the conclusions which necessarily come from them may well shock those who have not been in close touch with what has been going on in our schools during the past thirty years. I wish to make perfectly clear, however, that the aim of this book is not to recommend that American schools imitate Soviet schools; in fact, the following chapters will serve to point up some of the distortions of Soviet education. Rather, the aim is to show that these basic subjects are very poorly represented in the curriculum and textbooks of American schools even when compared to the curriculum and textbooks of the schools in a Communist country. How seriously American schools neglect the humanities can be even more readily demonstrated by a comparison between our curriculum and textbooks and those of Western European schools; but it seems vastly more significant to show that the curriculum and textbooks of the schools of a country governed by a philosophy which is commonly thought to suppress the humanities

7

and to stress technological education, do in fact provide far more thorough training in the humanities than the curriculum and textbooks of American schools. In other words, this book proposes to show that instruction in these basic subjects in American schools is poor by any standards. This is not, then, a book about Soviet schools; it is a book about American schools.

The intention of this book is not merely to lay bare some of the serious deficiencies of our schools, but to insist upon the importance of giving American students a thorough education in the humanities, and to make concrete, and, it is hoped, practical proposals for a dramatic improvement in the quality of American schools. These proposals are made not only so that our schools can make a greater contribution to rolling back the incursions of communism, but also so that the intellectual resources of our children and of America may be greatly strengthened for any eventuality.

Perhaps the most attractive feature of these proposals is that they can be executed without money. All that is needed is a little determination and hard work on the part of parents, teachers, school administrators, members of school boards, and all others who are concerned with improving the quality of our schools.

The basic source material used in this study consists of the textbooks and syllabi used in Soviet schools, a large number of textbooks used in American schools, and numerous authoritative and recently published studies on Soviet and American education. I wish to acknowledge my indebtedness to the U. S. Office of Education for its full co-operation in making available to me its reports on Soviet and American schools. The translations from the Russian are my own.

# 1

## READERS AND THE
## TEACHING OF READING
## IN SOVIET AND AMERICAN
## SCHOOLS

In a profound sense the reading program is the backbone of the curriculum of any school system. Perhaps no factor more strongly dictates the success of a student's academic career than his ability to comprehend the printed page. How much a student learns in school is, in fact, directly related to how well he can read. Not only history and geography and the sciences, but virtually every other academic subject that he studies demands that he read textbooks and other material—and he must be able to understand what he reads; otherwise, he will be handicapped in school and in later life as well.

Because of our increasing awareness of the importance of education in the struggle between communism and the free world, it seems particularly appropriate at this time to examine how well American schools measure up to the Soviet schools in the teaching of reading. I should like in this chapter, therefore, to make some comparisons between Soviet and American readers that are now being used in the first four grades, since it is primarily upon these readers that both school systems depend in teaching students to read.

Despite a great many language variations, students throughout the Soviet Union study pretty much the same material at each grade level. As a result, the textbooks used in Soviet schools are, with few exceptions, standardized in all subjects for all grades.

As examples of the printer's art they have little to recommend them, especially compared to American textbooks. They are virtually all the same size (6″ x 9″), and since they are also thin and lightweight they are easily manageable, but the paper is cheap, especially in texts for the upper grades, and they are cheaply and flimsily bound. Nor are the illustrations at all comparable either in quality or quantity to those in American texts, which commonly, and especially in the lower grades, have color illustrations on nearly every page. In the Soviet texts from the fifth grade up, the illustrations tend to be sparse and consist chiefly of carefully drawn but badly reproduced engravings or line drawings. It is interesting to note, too, that for better or for worse, Soviet texts tend to introduce normal-sized print and normal line-spacing as early as the third grade, whereas American texts commonly delay introducing normal print and especially normal line-spacing until the ninth or tenth grade.

The textbooks from which Soviet students are chiefly taught to read consist of a *bukvar,* or alphabet book, and a series of four readers called RODNAYA RECH (Native Language), one for each of the first four grades. On the whole, the format of these books is not unattractive. The *bukvar* is an over-sized book containing many colored pictures. The RODNAYA RECH readers also have a number of full-page color illustrations and numerous black and white illustrations. In the readers of the first two grades the print is large and highly readable.

The chief aim of the reading program in Soviet elementary schools is to teach students to read anything of moderate difficulty by the end of the fourth grade. In fact, in the fifth grade, as the next chapter will indicate, Soviet students begin a systematic study of Russian literature, and at that time they begin to read adult selections from some of Russia's best authors, often unaltered from the original.

Soviet students are taught to read according to a phonics system. They start out by learning from their *bukvar* all the letters of their Cyrillic alphabet and the sounds of these letters, alone and in various combinations, and they practice reading sentences and short paragraphs with a vocabularly of about 300 words. All this they do in a few weeks' time. They then proceed to their first-grade reader, which has some 130 selections and a vocabulary of about 2,000 words; but since they have already been thoroughly trained in the phonics of the Russian language, they are expected to have no great difficulty in handling a vocabulary so large.

Their second-grade reader is a somewhat larger book, with about 165 selections and a vocabulary of approximately 4,000 words. Their third-grade RODNAYA RECH reader is a formidable book indeed, and consists of 384 closely printed pages with relatively few illustrations and a vocabulary of 7,000 or 8,000 words. The fourth-grade RODNAYA RECH reader has fewer, but longer and considerably more difficult, selections—with a vocabulary of about 10,000 words.

It seems desirable to give some account of the contents of these readers, because many interesting—indeed, important—comparisons can be made between what Soviet students find in their readers and what American students find in theirs. As the ensuing description proceeds, the reader may wish to refer from time to time to the tables of contents of these readers as they have been translated and reproduced at the end of this chapter.

The selections in these RODNAYA RECH readers may be conveniently divided into four groups, as follows: (1) selections which are purely for purposes of Communist indoctrination; (2) exemplary selections, usually in a narrative style, which more or less pointedly exhort students to act or refrain from acting in one way or another and which are aimed at character building; (3) selections which are chiefly informational and which tend therefore to be expository rather than narrative in style; and (4) literary selections, including a large number of poems, which are often highly artistic and which sometimes, though not always, seem to have no other purpose than to instill in young students a love of reading and to develop their aesthetic sensibilities. Many selections, of course, attempt to perform two or three of these functions simultaneously. For example, a poem may be purely propagandistic, or a highly artistic story may be rather directly aimed at illustrating some virtue, or a selection written in a narrative style may be designed chiefly to convey factual information.

Selections intended as Communist indoctrination are sprinkled throughout Soviet readers in the early grades. In the closing pictures of his *bukvar*, the first-grade scholar is reassured that "The Communist Party resolutely leads the people along the Leninist path." He also finds there a large picture of Lenin, and he sharpens his reading skill on a few paragraphs that explain who Lenin was.

Most of the propaganda selections in the first-grade reader are concentrated in the short section called "In Lenin's Day." One of these selections, which is designed to illustrate that Lenin loved children, tells how Lenin visited an orphan's home, played some games with the children (including cat and mouse) and how Lenin's sister then brought in some toys which were distributed to the children amid squeals of delight. The story is accompanied by a full-page color illustration of Lenin sitting on a park bench with his arm around a little girl as he listens to a little boy who is standing in front of him and reciting from a book.

There is also a poem about a little boy and his sister exploring the wonders of the Lenin Museum. Still another selection, entitled "What the Legacy of Lenin Has Accomplished," describes how a large estate was inhabited before the Revolution by a rich landowner who had servants to do all the work, who forbade peasants and workers to enjoy his grounds, and who allowed only his own children to play in the garden, but how, after the Revolution, the estate was turned into an orphanage where fifty children were clothed, fed, schooled, and allowed to romp about the garden. This selection is accompanied by two half-page illustrations: one shows in pre-Revolutionary days an elegantly dressed dowager sitting on the porch, peering through a lorgnette into the garden, and flanked on either side by a pet dog and a table with a samovar and a tea service; the second illustration shows post-Revolutionary orphans swarming all over the same porch.

A large number of the selections in this first-grade reader are hortatory or exemplary in tone and intent. For example, the first section, entitled "School," has selections which urged students to like school, to be on time, to sit up straight at their desks, to let classmates do their own homework, and to study hard themselves. The section ends with a story by Leo Tolstoy about Little Philip, an underage boy who is so eager to be in school that one day he slips out of the house, runs through the village to the school, and bursts into the classroom where his brother is a student. He is allowed to stay when the teacher discovers that his older brother has already taught him to read.

Another section, entitled "The Family," has selections illustrating the love of a little girl for her mother, the pride a boy takes in his father, and the devotion of another boy to his little sister. One rather grotesque story called "Mama Is an Airplane Pilot" ends when a little girl who has expressed a desire to fly away with her mother in an airplane is confronted with her mother's question, "But who would look after Papa if we both flew away?" Whereupon the little girl agrees to stay behind.

Another story illustrates the error of stealing plums and especially of denying having stolen them, and another suggests that when an old woman stumbles and falls, it is well for little boys to help her up even though she may not be their grandmother. Elsewhere in the book there are stories urging children to wash every morning and evening, to keep their teeth clean always, to feed the birds in winter, to kill beetles in May because they eat the leaves of tender plants, not to kill hedgehogs at any time because they eat mice and snails, to consider the advantages of being a sailor, and to appreciate the miracle of the telephone and the wonders of the Moscow subway.

In the first-grade reader, selections which are primarily informational avoid the danger of a dull expository style which might blunt a young student's interest; as a result, most of them are in narrative or anecdotal form. A large number of selections, under general headings such as "The City," "Winter," "Spring," and "Domestic and Wild Animals," manage to dispense information about such subjects as: what can be found in Moscow, where and how squirrels spend the winter, why shadows vary in length at various times of the day, how bees live, which mushrooms are edible and which are not, and so on.

A fourth kind of selection that appears in this first-grade reader consists of a surprising number of genuinely artistic and literary pieces by famous Russian authors, most of whom are pre-Soviet, not Soviet, authors. For example, there are 2 anecdotes, 3 stories, one fable, and one fairy tale (a version of "The Three Bears") by Leo Tolstoy; there are 3 poems by Pushkin, one fable by Krylov, a poem by Nicholas Nekrassov and one by Lermontov. There are also a rather large number of anonymous tales, poems, stories, and particularly animal fables drawn from a rich Russian folklore tradition, and which have a distinct literary value. There are also a number of selections by well-known contemporary Soviet authors. Altogether, about one-third of the selections in the first-grade RODNAYA RECH reader have genuine literary merit, and some are written by Russia's greatest authors.

The second-grade reader in the RODNAYA RECH series (see the table of contents at the end of this chapter) is planned along the same lines as the first-grade reader, though the selections are noticeably more difficult. The selections intended for Communist indoctrination appear chiefly in the sections entitled "The Great October Socialist Revolution," "The Soviet Army," and "The Celebration of the First of May." The sections on wild and domestic animals, on the seasons, on the school, the family, and the city correspond to those in the first-grade reader.

Stories illustrating courage, bravery, self-sacrifice, and devotion to duty are rather common in this reader and throughout the series. Many of these are adventure stories and are often exciting. Purely informational selections are still rather rare, though there is some straightforward botany in the selections entitled "The Forest" and "The Kitchen Garden."

Again the literary value of many of the selections is considerable—about one-third of them contribute to the Soviet student's familiarity with his cultural heritage. Leo Tolstoy, Krylov, Pushkin, Nekrassov, Maikov, Lermontov, and Chekhov account for about 22 of these selections. In addition, there are many more folk tales and poems, dealing particularly with animals.

The third-grade reader in the RODNAYA RECH series is, as I have indicated, an imposing book. It is divided into three main parts: a literary section, a geography and nature section, and a history section. It may be noted that the "Literary Section" is indeed literary (see the table of contents at the end of this chapter). Thirty-five of the 77 selections are of established literary value, and only 5 of the 35 are by Soviet writers (Isakovsky and Alexei Tolstoy). Many of the other pre-Soviet selections are drawn from the Russian folk-tale tradition.

It will be noted that this reader contains a good many selections in the second and third sections that are primarily informational. Even some of these are by Russia's best authors. Some of them are cast in a narrative style, but many others are wholly expository and often rather technical. The section on the human body, for example, has discussions accompanied by diagrams and illustrations of the skeleton, the rib cage, the muscular system, the lungs, the digestive tract, and the heart. There are even illustrations of the way six different kinds of bacteria look under a microscope. There are also short biographies of famous Russian inventors and explorers. And as the table of contents for this reader also shows, the "History Section" has almost fifty selections dealing with important events of Russia's past.

The fourth-grade RODNAYA RECH reader, as the table of contents reprinted at the end of this chapter indicates, retains many of the sections, such as those dealing with the seasons and the family, of the earlier readers; and although beginning in the fourth grade, history is taught as a separate subject with a separate textbook, there is also in the reader a section entitled "From Our Country's Past," and another called "The People of the Soviet Countries," which include additional historical and geographical material.

Selections for Communist indoctrination are not rare in this reader, and as the table of contents shows, students encounter three of them in the opening pages of the book. The final section, moreover, also has some selections which further apprise Soviet students of the activities of Lenin. But of the 84 selections in this book, a good many are by pre-Soviet authors, the most frequently represented of whom are Pushkin, Nekrassov, Krylov, and Turgenev. In addition there appear in various places in the book biographical sketches of such famous authors as Pushkin, Herzen, Nekrassov, Gorky, and Lomonosov. When the anonymous Russian folk tales and poems and selections from the better Soviet authors are added to these, it turns out that about half the selections in the fourth-grade RODNAYA RECH reader have true literary distinction.

These observations cannot provide a full picture of what the RODNAYA RECH readers are like, but they will perhaps serve to make what appear to be some crucial comparisons with the readers widely used in the United States in the first four grades of our schools, both public and parochial.

From what sort of readers, then, do our children learn to read in the first four grades of American elementary schools? No uniformity of textbooks is imposed upon American schools as it is upon Soviet schools; but unfortunately, as we shall see, there is a strong tendency for textbooks in any given subject at any given grade level to resemble one another so closely that there is often little to choose from among them.

This sameness is perhaps nowhere so evident as among elementary school readers. It is true that there are a large number of so-called "supplementary readers" on the market which vary widely in quality but which include many good readers and some excellent ones. However, though they are used in varying degrees, depending upon the school, they remain largely, as their name implies, "supplementary."

The core of the reading program of the overwhelming majority of public and parochial schools in this country is a series of carefully graded readers commonly referred to as "basal" readers. A fairly large number of these basal reading series are currently available. The most elaborate ones and in general the most widely used ones run through at least the sixth grade and some through the eighth grade, usually with a reader for each semester in the early grades. Some even include a special reader series for slow learners, and most of them also include a string of primers and pre-primers. The following list accounts for most of the basal reader series that run through at least the sixth grade which are now on the market:

ALICE AND JERRY BASIC READING PROGRAM, grades 1-6 (Row, Peterson and Company)

NEW BASIC READING PROGRAM, grades 1-8 (Scott, Foresman and Company)

BETTS BASIC READERS, grades 1-6 (American Book Company)

CATHEDRAL BASIC READING PROGRAM, grades 1-8 (Scott, Foresman and Company)

CRABTREE BASIC SERIES, grades 1-6 (University Publishing Company)

DEVELOPMENTAL READING SERIES, grades 1-8 (Lyons and Carnahan)

EASY GROWTH IN READING SERIES, grades 1-6 (John C. Winston Company)

FAITH AND FREEDOM READERS, grades 1-8 (Ginn and Company)

GINN BASIC READERS, grades 1-8 (Ginn and Company)

GOLDEN RULE SERIES, grades 1-8 (American Book Company)

LAIDLAW READERS ENRICHMENT SERIES, grades 1-8 (Laidlaw Brothers)

LEARNING TO READ, grades 1-6 (Silver Burdett Company)

MACMILLAN READERS SERIES, grades 1-8 (The Macmillan Company)

READING FOR INTEREST SERIES, grades 1-6 (D. C. Heath and Company)

READING FOR MEANING, grades 1-8 (Houghton Mifflin Company)

SHELDON BASIC READING SERIES, grades 1-8 (Allyn and Bacon, Inc.)

Despite the variety that this list may seem to suggest, all of these reader series, and a number of others which run only through the third grade, resemble one another in some important ways: (1) in the size of the vocabulary, (2) in the vocabulary-control apparatus, and (3) in the kind of reading selections which they contain. Each of these three aspects of American elementary readers warrants comparison with those of the RODNAYA RECH readers.

Perhaps the most salient fact about the vocabulary of these readers is that the vast majority of them for the first four grades introduce only 300 or 400 new words in each grade, so that whereas the first-grade RODNAYA RECH reader has a 2,000-word vocabulary, most American first-grade readers have a vocabulary that does not exceed the vocabulary of a Soviet student's alphabet book. Similarly, whereas the fourth-grade RODNAYA

RECH reader has a vocabulary approaching 10,000 words, most American fourth-grade readers have a vocabulary of well under 1,800 words.

It is true that American first graders are usually only six years old, whereas Soviet first graders are almost always seven, but in the matter of reading, American elementary students do not gain from starting a year earlier because, as we have seen, Soviet first graders learn the alphabet and phonics of their language and learn some 300 words from their *bukvar* in a matter of weeks. Therefore, first-grade Soviet readers very quickly give first-grade Soviet students an opportunity to over-take American second-grade students in reading vocabulary.

There is a marked discrepancy, too, between the sheer number of words that appear in the typical American reader series and in the RODNAYA RECH readers. One popular and typical American reader series, for example, supplies the information that the running word total of the entire series through the fourth grade is 66,071 words. By contrast, the running word total in the RODNAYA RECH series through the third grade is well over twice that number. In fact, the third-grade RODNAYA RECH reader alone has nearly twice that number.

One reason that the vocabulary and the total number of words in American elementary readers are small is that they are largely predicated upon the assumption that our children will be taught to read by the "whole-word" method or the "sight" method or the "look-and-say" method, as it is variously called. This method requires that students memorize each word by the way it looks on the page, much as Chinese students must learn Chinese ideographs. It was first introduced into the schools some thirty years ago, and is now in widespread use, though it is usually accompanied by a procedure of introducing the sounds of the letters at the rate of one or two a month over a period of two, three or even four years. There is a limit to the number of words that even a bright child can learn when he is not taught the sounds of the individual letters of a word but is rather made to memorize the way each one looks on the page.

There are also other strict rules of vocabulary control in these basic readers besides the practice of introducing only three or four hundred words at each grade level. One such rule is that all the words should be taken from certain approved "basic word lists" or "core-vocabulary lists," which are highly restrictive. Another is that only one or two or, in the more daring readers, three new words are permitted to appear on any given page. Still another is that each word has to be repeated somewhere in the reader a certain number of times, at least five and preferably ten times, and the more times it can be repeated on the same page the better. These last two rules are in recognition of the fact that students can memorize only a few words at a time by the "whole-word" method, and then only when they have seen them repeatedly.

Sometimes these rules of vocabulary control are downright exquisite. One widely used reader, for example, explains in the back pages that the maximum number of new words introduced per sentence is one; per page, two; per story, eight; per "activity," two; and that the maximum total words per sentence is fifteen. Other readers make a point of not introducing any more new words than are absolutely necessary. One second-grade reader states that there are "113 pages with no new words." Another widely used first-grade reader states that one of the purposes of the book is "to keep the introduction of new words to a minimum" and that in the last 137 pages of the book "no new words are introduced."

All of these rules naturally do much to determine the nature of the selections which appear in these readers. But there is also one other major consideration which accounts for the kind of selections that they contain. I refer to a highly influential theory of education which proposes that the schools must teach students to adapt themselves to their immediate community environment. But it is a bit ironic that the environment commonly represented in these readers is an oversimplified, exclusively middle-class idealization, almost always unrelated to real life—a fact which even many children can readily perceive.

The selections in elementary school readers, particularly for the first two or three grades, consist chiefly of little stories which take place very close to home and preferably at home. One reader, which is fairly typical, describes this policy as follows: "The story content portrays children carrying on everyday activities, gradually extending their experiences in both home and community. It emphasizes typical neighborhood conditions, with children of different characteristics playing and working together." As a result, the selections in elementary school readers for the early grades deal chiefly with cardboard boys and girls who participate in trivial episodes involving mommies and daddies, baby sisters and visiting aunts, grandfathers who own farms, mailmen, corner cops and corner grocers, and other assorted people in a hypothetical and sterilized community.

It is no easy matter to write exciting or even interesting stories which have a vocabulary of only a few hundred pre-chosen words, which introduce only a few new words on each page, which repeat them frequently, and which impose severe limitations in setting and scope. They are likely to turn out like this one from a typical elementary school primer:

### Little Rabbit

"Alice, Alice!" said Jerry.
"Come here! Come here!
I see something brown."
Alice looked down.
She saw something little.
She saw something brown.
She saw a little brown rabbit.
"Oh, look, Jerry," said Alice.
Little Rabbit saw Jerry.
She saw Alice, too.

Hop went the rabbit.
Hop, hop, hop!
Alice and Jerry ran and ran.
Little Rabbit saw something.
She saw a hole.
A little brown rabbit hole!
Down, down she went.
"Oh!" said Alice and Jerry.

I had hoped to cite other examples, but some publishers have not granted permission to reproduce material from their books. The reader may draw whatever conclusions he will to account for the publishers' reluctance. The following two examples represent my own attempt to approximate the sort of material that regularly appears in elementary texts. To realize that I have not exaggerated, the reader is invited to look at copies of such actual texts as the first-grade reader of the NEW BASIC READING PROGRAM.

This might be from a typical first-grade reader:

### Up and Down

"See me go, Betty," said Fred.
"See me go down."
"I am going down the hill on my sled."
"Down, down I go on my big red sled."
But Betty did not see Fred go down.
Betty was going up.
Up, up, up the hill she went, pulling her little blue sled.
"Here I come, too," said Betty.
"I am going down too."
"I am going down on my little blue sled."
"Down, down, down, I go."
"I like to go down better than up," said Betty.
"I do too," said Fred. "I like to go down too. I do not like to go up."

And this might be from a typical second-grade reader:

22

### A Trip to the Grocery Store

Mother said to Lucy, "Lucy, will you go to the store for me?"

"Yes, Mother," said Lucy. "I will go to the store for you. I like to go to the store."

"I am baking a cake," said Mother, "and I have no sugar. Bring back five pounds of sugar. Here is the money. Don't lose the change."

Mother gave Lucy a dollar bill, and Lucy ran off to the store.

"Hello, Lucy," said Jolly George, the grocer. "Where did you get all that money?"

"My mother gave it to me to buy sugar with," said Lucy. "I want five pounds of sugar."

"That is a lot of sugar for one little girl," said Jolly George.

"Oh, the sugar is not for me," laughed Lucy. "It is for my mother. She is baking a cake."

"Oh, I see," laughed Jolly George. "There you are, and here is your change. Don't lose your change."

"Oh, I won't," said Lucy, and away she ran until she reached home.

"Here is the sugar and the change," said Lucy to her mother.

"Oh, thank you, thank you," said Mother. "What a big, big little girl you are!"

If one multiplies these stories by fifteen or twenty he will have a fair idea of the nature of most first- and second-grade readers used in American schools. Beginning with the stories that appear in the third-grade readers, there is greater variety in setting and approach; but it is still pretty hard to do much with only a thousand- or a fifteen-hundred-word vocabulary, especially when the words have to be repeated ever so often and when only one or two new ones are permitted on each page.

It seems pertinent, finally, to make some comparisons between the kinds of selections which appear in American and Soviet readers by a consideration of the questions I have discussed in connection with the RODNAYA RECH series. Do these American basal readers instill a particular attitude toward our country? Do they contain selections which are aimed at the moral development of our children? Do they contain selections that are primarily informational? And, finally, do they contain selections which have literary value? I should like to deal with these first three questions briefly and with the last one at more length.

In the pages at the end of this chapter, I have printed the tables of contents of a number of the most widely used basal readers ranging from grades one through four, and have placed them directly facing the tables of contents of the corresponding RODNAYA RECH readers. Although the titles of the selections do not always give a good idea of the content, they do much to indicate the general nature of these books, and the reader is invited to make his own comparisons as this discussion proceeds. In order to make allowances for the fact that Soviet students are a year older than American students at any given grade level, the reader may feel that comparing the contents of a Soviet reader with those of an American reader one grade higher is more equitable.

Selections in the RODNAYA RECH readers not only try to impress upon students the importance of the Communist Revolution, the glorious leadership of the Communist Party in general and of Lenin in particular, but they also exhort students to live for communism, to work for communism, and to make all manner of sacrifices for communism. These readers also continually exhort Soviet students to love their country, to love its people, to appreciate its greatness and its beauty, and to learn more about its past.

By way of contrast and without attempting a judgment, I should like to point out simply as a fact that the vast majority of the basal readers used in our schools in the first four grades have no selections devoted to praising the virtues of the democratic way of life, or which invite young students to consider

24

how fortunate they are to live in a free country. Nor can one easily find selections in these readers which encourage students to love their country, to appreciate its greatness or its beauty, or to learn about its past, or which even remind them of what country they live in.

We have seen too that the RODNAYA RECH readers contain numerous selections exhorting students to work hard, to study hard, to be willing to make sacrifices, to be brave, to love and obey their parents, to be clean, and to be kind to old ladies and animals. The dominance of secularism in this country has prevented American basal readers, except those designed for parochial schools, from being concerned with spiritual values, but many selections in some readers are aimed directly or indirectly at the student's moral development. The GOLDEN RULE series and the FAITH AND FREEDOM series, for example, are full of selections of this sort.

Many of these basal readers also present ethical questions in an artificially simple light. There are many stories, usually animal stories, which stress, for example, that children should not try to be or do something they are not or cannot do, that they should share their candy and be otherwise considerate of others, and that they should not be different from the members of their peer group.

But unlike the RODNAYA RECH readers, dramatic representations of such manly virtues as bravery and devotion to duty are rather scarce in American readers for the early grades, and the policy of limiting the stories to settings that are close to home not only prevents much in the way of genuine excitement or high adventure, but also thereby automatically rules out a good amount of the best literature for young people. And it must be observed finally that many of the stories in these readers of the first four grades are to an excruciating degree insipid, trivial, inane, pointless, and otherwise devoid of either pleasure or profit.

We have seen that the informational value of the selections

in the RODNAYA RECH series is considerable, especially in the third- and fourth-grade readers. Here, the contrast between American and Soviet readers is marked. In the first place, expository writing in American readers of the early grades is very rare, so that whatever of an informational nature is in these readers is buried in a story of some sort, and consequently the information actually is superficial, slight, and incidental. Furthermore, it is not easy to be very informative when one has only 1,000 or 1,500 words to work with, especially when only one or two new words can appear on each page. Some, though not many, fifth- and sixth-grade readers do have selections which are informational, but they tend to run heavily to cowboy and Indian lore and thus often do little more than supplement the information to be had from watching TV Westerns. I know of no American reader series through the fourth grade that has an informational section at all comparable in importance to the geography and history section in the third-grade RODNAYA RECH reader (see the tables of contents at the end of this chapter).

What, finally, is the literary or artistic value of the typical American reader series for the first four grades? It is no exaggeration to say that it is negligible. To be specific, some of the most widely used basal reader series among those listed on pages 17-18 are the NEW BASIC READING PROGRAM, ALICE AND JERRY READING PROGRAM, READING FOR LIVING, EASY GROWTH IN READING SERIES, SHELDON BASIC READING SERIES, and BETTS BASIC READERS. These, or indeed, any other combination of American readers listed on pages 17-18 will serve to indicate the lack of genuinely artistic pieces in the typical reader series.

None of the first-year readers of these six series has a vocabulary exceeding 400 words, and taken together the first-year readers in these series yield a grand total of two selections written by recognizable authors: namely, Robert Louis Stevenson's twelve-line poem "Bed in Summer," and a revamped version of a tale by Joel Chandler Harris. The only other selections that can possibly be said to have any literary merit whatsoever are two old folk tales. Four of these six first-grade readers have nothing of any literary value at all.

Nor is there any notable advance in the literary quality of the selections in the second-grade readers. The second-grade reader for the NEW BASIC series has eight assorted fairy and folk tales; the BETTS BASIC READERS book has five such tales and a story by Phyllis McGinley, but nothing else that is to any degree literary. The DEVELOPMENTAL READING SERIES reader, to mention another, has a story by Mark Van Doren, a Grimm fairy tale, and an excerpt from Longfellow's *Hiawatha,* which, however, is "to be read *to* the children" (italics mine), not *by* the children. The second reader in the ALICE AND JERRY books does not have anything of literary significance at all, nor does the one in the EASY GROWTH IN READING SERIES or the one in the SHELDON BASIC READING SERIES.

Whatever literary selections appear in the typical third-grade reader used in American schools rarely reach beyond the anonymous, and usually adapted, folk-tale level. The third-grade reader for the NEW BASIC READERS has a dozen more of these tales, or about a sixth of the total text, but nothing else of literary significance. The reader in the READING FOR LIVING series has four such tales, and the BETTS BASIC READERS book for the third grade also has four. The third-grade reader for the SHELDON BASIC READING SERIES has nothing of literary significance except an Anderson fairy tale. The one in the ALICE AND JERRY books has nothing of literary value whatsoever, nor does that in the DEVELOPMENTAL READING SERIES; and, to add three more to the list, the third-grade readers for the EASY GROWTH IN READING SERIES, for the READING FOR MEANING series, and for the FAITH AND FREEDOM series also contain nothing that can be considered literary.

Even the number of literary selections in widely used fourth-grade readers in American elementary schools is negligible. The fourth-year reader in the NEW BASIC series has one selection apiece by Cornelia Meigs, Carl Sandburg, and Dr. Seuss. The DEVELOPMENTAL READING SERIES book for the fourth grade has a piece by Cornelia Meigs and one old tale. The one in the ALICE AND JERRY books has nothing whatsoever of literary value nor does that in the EASY GROWTH IN READING series.

It should be emphasized too that the recognizable writers who do appear in American elementary readers for these grades are not among the first ranks of American or English writers; in fact, most of them are in the fifth or sixth ranks and an overwhelming majority of authors whose names appear opposite the selections listed in the table of contents of these readers are by unimaginative or unknown children's writers who know all about the rules of vocabulary control. One basal reader series even says as much: "The selections . . . were written or adapted by authors all of whom have had many years of experience with the vocabularies of the various 'word lists' and of all types of children's literature. The frequencies or ratings of words in the Gates Vocabulary, the Thorndike and the Thorndike-Lorge Word Lists, and the Rinsland and the Dale vocabulary studies were taken into account. To illustrate: Any word not appearing in the Thorndike or Thorndike-Lorge or Rinsland lists was given careful scrutiny and another more common synonym chosen when . . . it was deemed more useful."

It should come as no great surprise, then, that the selections in American elementary readers are almost wholly nonliterary. The reader may imagine, for example, that no small poem by Shakespeare or Wordsworth, or even Eugene Field, who knew nothing about the rules of vocabulary control, could bear the scrutiny described above. Occasionally, as I have noted, a familiar poem does creep in, but it appears there usually because of the recklessness of the editors, who admit sometimes in small print in the back of the book that the poem violates the rules of vocabulary control.

I should like very much to be able to say that there is available among American basal readers a series with selections even remotely comparable in difficulty, in literary quality, and in informational value to those in the RODNAYA RECH readers, but I know of none. About the best one can say of these basal readers is that some are worse than others; but not much worse, because they are all bad.

I do not wish to imply here that no elementary school children learn to read well by the end of the fourth grade, because fortunately many students do not depend upon their readers to learn to read. Some students are taught to read at home, others are encouraged by their teachers to read many supplementary books, while others simply love to read and increase their skill by reading at every opportunity. Obviously many students learn to read well by the end of the fourth grade, but it is just as obvious that they do not learn to read well from their basal readers. No students can acquire a vocabulary of more than 1,500 words from a fourth-grade reader that has a vocabulary of no more than 1,500 words.

There can be no question, then, that all students who are taught to read from these basal readers are being seriously shortchanged. Most students begin to study history and geography and science in the fourth grade, and if the texts for these subjects are good texts, they are bound to have a vocabulary of between 6,000 and 8,000 words; and yet fourth-grade students inherit a reading knowledge of only about 1,000 words from their third-grade readers. One wonders how many students really succeed in overcoming the handicap which these basal readers place them under in learning other subjects. But parents who find that their children are poor readers or are otherwise doing poorly in school would do well indeed to suspect first not their children's intelligence or eyesight or nervous system, or their teachers, but their readers.

# First-Grade Soviet Reader

*Title:* RODNAYA RECH (Native Language)
*Vocabulary:* Approximately 2000 words

> NOTE: This and the RODNAYA RECH readers for the following three grades are used by all Soviet students, not merely the bright students

## CONTENTS

*(Pre-Soviet authors are given in parentheses)*

### I. SCHOOL

How Lenin Learned; The Way to School and from School; Guess What This Is; Our Class; School Supplies; Everything in Its Place; Joke; How to Sit in Class; For the Student to Remember (*poem*); A Real Friend; Little Philip (*story by Leo Tolstoy*)

### II. THE FAMILY

Best of All; A Mother's Song; My Mother; My Son; Grandma Vera; Mama Is an Airplane Pilot; A Remarkable Man; My Sister; Sleep, My Beautiful Boy (*lullaby by Mikhail Lermontov*); The Plum Pit (*story by Leo Tolstoy*); The Helpers; The Old Woman

### III. WINTER

The Outdoor Boy (*poem by Alexander Pushkin*); A Guest at Uncle Frost's; Winter Twilight (*poem by Nicholas Nekrassov*); The Man Under the Snow; Reflections in the Window; The

# First-Grade American Reader

*Title:* Open Windows
*Series:* GOLDEN RULE SERIES
*Publisher:* American Book Company
*Authors:* Mary Louise Friebele and others

*From "Vocabulary Information" (printed in the back of the book)*

"This first reader contains 158 new words, exclusive of proper names. . . . A word is counted as new if it is not in the American Book Company Core Vocabulary for Use in First Readers. This Core Vocabulary is composed of words common to at least five out of eight series of basic pre-primers and primers. Poems are excluded from the vocabulary control."

| | |
|---|---|
| Maximum new words per sentence | 1 |
| Maximum new words per page | 2 |
| Maximum new words per story | 8 |
| Maximum new words per activity | 2 |
| Maximum words per sentence | 15 |

## STORIES IN THIS BOOK

### AT PLAY

Stories *by Mary Louise Friebele:* The Circus; The Blue and Yellow Boats; The Dime; A Funny Sled

### AT SCHOOL

Stories *by Mary Louise Friebele:* I Can't Find It; Lunch for Bobby; At the Bus Stop; One and Two, and Then Comes Three

### AT HOME

Stories *by Mary Louise Friebele:* All by Myself; In a Minute; A Good, Big Fire; Jack's New Train; Sleepy Head (*poem by Lee Mountain*)

Sparrows; Winter (*poem*); What Woodpeckers Eat in the Winter; Winter in the Forest; The Jackdaw (*poem*); My Rabbit; The Two Frost Brothers; The Small Round Loaf (*fairy tale*)

#### IV.  IN LENIN'S DAY

The Yule Tree in Sokolny; In the Lenin Museum (*poem*); What the Legacy of Lenin Has Accomplished

#### V.  THE SOVIET ARMY

February (*poem*); A Parade (*poem*); I Want to Be Such a Sailor; We Are for Peace (*poem*); A March; The Shaggy Hospital Attendant (*i.e., a dog*)

#### VI.  THE CITY

The Kremlin Stars (*poem*); Arrival in Moscow; The Traffic Light; The Moscow-Soviet in Moscow Is the Master; Concerning Wonderful Things; Wonderful Things at Home; The Moscow Subway (*poem*); The Wonderful Stairway (*i.e., the escalator*); Where the Streetcars and Buses Spend the Night; How Tim Mailed a Letter; The Firehouse Dog (*story by Leo Tolstoy*); The Fire (*poem*); In a Shoe Factory

#### VII.  BE CLEAN AND YOU WILL BE HEALTHY

Why Bathing is Necessary (*poem*); How You Should Wash and Clean Your Teeth; What Is Good and What Is Bad (*poem*)

### AT WORK

Something to Wait For (*by Katheryne Hitte*); One Little Indian (*by Mary Louise Friebele*); Enough for Everyone (*by Mary Louise Friebele*); Mother's Helper—Father's Helper (*poem by Lee Mountain*); Who Gets It (*by Marion Mitchelson Gartler*); Because I'm Happy (*prayer by Edna Hull Miller*)

### AT PARTY TIME

What George Forgot (*by Marion Mitchelson Gartler*); The Pony Party (*by Mary Louise Friebele*)

### AT STORY TIME

Daniel; The Boy Who Cried Wolf (*from the McGuffey Third Reader*); The King Who Could not Smile (*by Hazel M. Kulik*); The Other Way Around (*by Moritz Jagendorf*)

33

VIII.  DOMESTIC AND WILD ANIMALS

The Little Darling; The Sorrel and the Wolf; A Joke; The Kostroma Cows; Byryonyshka (*folk song*); Sheep; The Two Goats; The Little Pigs; The Puppy; The Quarrel of the Animals (*fairy tale*); Vaska the Tom Cat; Who Is More Frightening; The Mouse and the Rat; The Hare and the Hedgehog; The Little Hedgehog; How the Squirrel Spends the Winter; The Wonderful Squirrel (*poem by Alexander Pushkin*); The Fox; The Fox and the Mouse (*anecdote by Leo Tolstoy*); The Fox Plays Dead; The Wolf; The Fox and the Grouse (*fairy tale*); The Cat, the Cock, and the Fox (*fairy tale*); The Goat and the Wolf; The Goat (*fairy tale*); The Fox and the Crane (*fairy tale*); The Three Bears (*fairy tale by Leo Tolstoy*)

IX.  SPRING

March (*poem*); Toward Spring; Beautiful Spring; The Garden in the Little Window; The Bird House; Birds Are Our Friends; Spring (*poem*); The Rooks Arrive; The Hare Sheds Its Winter Coat; The Fox, the Hare, and the Cock (*fairy tale*); The Flood in the Forest; The Ice Moves; April (*poem*); The Festival of the Trees; Spring in the City (*poem*); The Cow and the Jackdaw; The Swallow (*poem*); The Swallows Return; The May Beetle; The Brooding Hen; The Ducks; The Geese; The Sun and the Rainbow; The Morning Rays; The Ant Hill; The Pond on the Collective Farm; The Bee on Reconaissance; The Flower Bed in the Little Window; Spring on a Collective Farm; Song of the Tractor Driver; The Medal; The Kitchen Garden; The Welcome Shower; Objects for Determining the Weather; Sparrows on the Watch; The Gardener and His Sons (*fable by Leo Tolstoy*); Four Wishes; The Sapling; On the Clear Lake; The Little Flag; A Lucky Day; The First of May; High in the Sky

## X.  SUMMER

The Housekeeper; My Little Garden; The Great Horticulturist;
The Sun and the Wind (*anecdote by Leo Tolstoy*); The Wind
(*poem by Alexander Pushkin*); Mushrooms; A Hot Summer

# Second-Grade Soviet Reader

*Title:* RODNAYA RECH (Native Language)
*Vocabulary:* Approximately 4000 words

## CONTENTS

*(Pre-Soviet authors are given in parentheses)*

# Second-Grade American Reader

*Title: People on Parade*
*Series:* WINSTON BASIC READERS
*Publisher:* The John C. Winston Company
*Authors:* R. G. Stauffer, A. T. Burrows, and others

### From "Vocabulary Facts" (*printed in the back of the book*)

"*People on Parade,* the second of two second readers in the WINSTON BASIC READER SERIES, introduces 189 new words. It re-presents the 498 words introduced in earlier books of the series. . . . No more than two new words are introduced on a page. No words are introduced in a story or unit title. Each new word is used five times or more in the story in which it is introduced and in the following story. At least one of these five uses is in the second of the two stories. The new words are maintained by being used a minimum of nine times in the book."

## CONTENTS

### IV. SCHOOL, FAMILY, COMRADES

In School (*poem*); A Teacher; What Is a Collective?; A Father and His Sons (*fable by Leo Tolstoy*); Blue Leaves; The Swan; The Crayfish and the Pike; The Siskin and the Dove; The Compote; Conscience; The Persistent Mr. Yun Soo; Lullaby (*by Apollon Maikov*); And What Do You Have?; Cucumbers; On the March; The Shark; Geese; The Magic Word

### V. THE GREAT OCTOBER SOCIALIST REVOLUTION

October (*poem*); How the Workers Lived Before the Soviets; How the Peasants Lived Before the Soviets; Vladimir Ilych Lenin; On the River Shush; An Autumn Sunset (*poem*); At Break of Day (*poem*); The Building; The Postal Factory; The Postman; The Airways; On the Street; Moscow Flowers; Mama's Work; Real Friends; The Painter (*poem*); The New City (*Nicholas Nekrassov*); How They Clean the City (*poem*)

### VI. WINTER

First Snow (*poem by Anton Chekhov*); A Winter Morning (*poem by Alexander Pushkin*); The Mischief of Old Man Winter (*fairy tale*); Winter Snowstorm; What Happens When; Childhood; The Ice Maiden (*fairy tale*); The Titmouse; Birds Under the Snow; In Winter; On a Block of Ice; In Winter on the Road; Old Father Time (*fairy tale*); The Fir Tree (*poem*); The Skiers (*poem*); In the Lenin Mountains

### VII. GETTING ACQUAINTED WITH OUR FIVE SENSES

Who Has Eyes in His Fingers?; Eyes and Ears; How Animals Look After Themselves; Our School Medical Attendant; A Fairy Tale

38

### DOWN THE ROAD

A New Grandfather; The Rainbow River Story; The True Story; Grandfather Gets Help; The Magic Words; A Mouse in the House

### ROUND AND ROUND

Tom's Trouble; A Few Good Things; Call the Police; Little (*poem*); King Take-Away; Merry-go-round (*poem*); Aunt Virginia's Surprise; The Lost Deer; A Little Squirrel (*poem*); The Rain (*poem*)

### MAKE BELIEVE

Old Moon Magic; Strange Work; Exciting Books; Once, in a Faraway Land; Big Feet; Tomorrow May Be Better; The Big Find; Never Stop Trying

None of these selections are signed but the "acknowledgments" state that the stories have been adapted from works of the following writers: Laura Arlon; Clyde Robert Bulla; Harriet Eager Davis; Grace Nies Fletcher; Marion E. Gridley; Franklin P. Harry; Fleur Conkling Heylinger; Jessie Holtzhaurer; Mildred B. Lissfelt; Mickey Klar Marks; Martha Murphy; Myrtle Gillespie Potter; Mabel Watts; Jeanne Barstow; and Marie Bloch.

## VIII.  THE SOVIET ARMY

The Soviet Soldier (*poem*); Vanya Andriavov; Never Forget (*poem*); Partisan Tonya; Our Native Land (*poem*); On Parade (*poem*)

## IX.  DOMESTIC AND WILD ANIMALS

Bulka (*story by Leo Tolstoy*); How a Dog Sought His Friend; The Horse; The Beloved Horse of Bydyonnovo; The Horse (*poem by Alexander Pushkin*); The Butting Cow; How Wolves Teach Their Children (*by Leo Tolstoy*); The Cat and the Squirrel; The Wolf and the Cat (*fable by Ivan Krylov*); The Fox and the Gray Wolf; The Brave Hare (*by Dimitri Mamin-Sibiryak*); How the Cock Deceived the Fox (*folk tale*); Masha and the Bear (*folk tale*); On What Kind of Animals People Travel; How an Elephant Saved His Master from a Tiger; The Lion; The Tiger; The Animals in the Circus

## X.  SPRING

The End of Winter (*poem*); A Spring Thaw (*poem by Alexander Pushkin*); Spring on a Collective Farm; The Skylark (*poem*); The Starling; How Birds Build Their Nests; The Spring Sowing; Morning (*poem by Alexander Pushkin*); The Little Sparrow (*folk tale*); A Story About a Sparrow and a Ruff (*by Dimitri Mamin-Sibiryak*); The Golden Meadow

## XI.  THE FOREST

The Quarrel of the Trees; The Birch Tree; The Birch; The Fir Tree; The Lime Tree; How the Forest Helps the Harvest; The Forest; The Cherry Tree (*poem*); The Apple Tree; Who Ruined the Apple Crop; The Most Important

## XII. THE CELEBRATION OF THE
### FIRST OF MAY

The Field Grass Appears (*poem*); A Holiday on Board Ship; A May Day Song; The First of May in 1905; The First of May (*poem*); The Celebration of Victory; Victory (*poem*); Reformers of Nature; An Evening Conversation, A Great Problem; How the Volga Came as a Guest; The Children of Free China

# Third-Grade Soviet Reader

*Title:* RODNAYA RECH (Native Language)
*Vocabulary:* Approximately 8000 words

## CONTENTS

*(Pre-Soviet authors are given in parentheses)*

### I. LITERARY SECTION

RECOLLECTIONS OF SUMMER: Beautiful Summer; Farewell to Summer (*poem*); In the Forest (*by Maxim Gorky*); The Peasant Children (*poem by Nicholas Nekrassov*); An Adventure in the Forest (*by Leo Tolstoy*); The Dawn (*poem*); The Mower (*poem*); In Summer (*poem*); The Bathing Bear; Mushrooms (*poem*); Echo (*poem by Nicholas Nekrassov*)

AUTUMN: The Birds Migrate (*poem*); Autumn; The Swans (*by Leo Tolstoy*); Farewell to the Warm Summer; The Old Man and the Swan (*by Dimitri Mamin-Sibiryak*); The Foster Child; Autumn (*poem*); Autumn Observations; On a Collective Farm in Autumn; Why the Pine Trees Didn't Grow

SCHOOL, COMRADES, FAMILY: Song of Soviet School Boys; The First Student; A Letter to Children; The Banner of Lenin; The Pioneer; The Soldier's Knife; the Pioneer Necktie; A Conversation; My Childhood Friends (*by Maxim Gorky*); Yanka the Musician; Three Friends; The Jump (*by Leo Tolstoy*); Word of Honor; Natasha; In a New Family; Lenin's Childhood and School Years

WINTER: Frost (*poem by Nicholas Nekrassov*); The Hare (*by Leo Tolstoy*); Winter Wind (*poem by Alexander Pushkin*); Winter Road (*poem by Alexander Pushkin*); In a Snowstorm; Ours and Mine; General Toptigin (*by Nicholas Nekrassov*); The Dog with the White Forehead (*by Anton Chekhov*)

# Third-Grade American Reader

*Title: This Is Our Valley*
*Series:* FAITH AND FREEDOM READERS
*Publishers:* Ginn and Company
*Authors:* Sister Mary Marguerite and others

*From "To the Teacher" (printed in the back of the book)*

"A large percentage of the vocabulary introduced in the preceding books of the series is repeated and maintained throughout this book, as well as the 401 new words introduced in the text."

## CONTENTS

FAIRY TALES AND FABLES: The Wolf and the Crane (*fable by Ivan Krylov*); The Cat and the Fox (*folk tale*); The Cat, the Donkey, and the Sheep (*Russian folk tale*); The Curious One (*fable by Ivan Krylov*); The Fox and the Grapes (*fable by Ivan Krylov*); The Elephant and the Pug Dog (*fable by Ivan Krylov*); The Story of the Fisherman and the Fish (*by Alexander Pushkin*); The Marmoset and the Spectacles (*fable by Ivan Krylov*)

SPRING: The Land Shows Itself; The Melting of the Last Snow; Spring (*by Leo Tolstoy*); On the Threshold of Spring; Uncle Mazai and the Hares (*by Nicholas Nekrassov*); The Story of Mother Olga; Fires in the Steppes; Spring (*poem*); The Neighbors Helped; The Ugly Duckling (*fairy tale by Hans Christian Anderson*); A Spring Thunderstorm; The Airplane; The Green Riot (*by Nicholas Nekrassov*); The First of May; Then and Now; The First of May (*poem*)

CITIES AND ROADS: Song about Moscow; Moscow; A Song about the Subway; The Marble City under Moscow; How I Became a Machinist; The Son (*poem*); At the Pole; The Sea and the Sailors (*poem*)

## II. GEOGRAPHY AND NATURAL SCIENCE SECTION

FINDING ONE'S LOCATION: How I Observed the Sun; The Horizon; What Is a Plan; Mapping a Plot of Land; The Commander's Map; How Masha Found His Way in the Forest; The Compass

THE FIELDS: A Collective Farm Harvest (*poem*); Grain Plants; The Farmer's Worst Enemy; War in the Grain Field; Four-footed Enemies of the Harvest; Trapping Gophers; Let's Take Care of the Birds; Cotton; The Sarafan-Maker (*poem*)

DOMESTIC ANIMALS: A Boy and His Horse; The Giant Horses; Pasha the Calf; The Soviet People Are Producing More Milk; The Camel; A Conversation on the Porch (*poem*)

THE GARDEN: Ivan Michurin (*horticulturist*); The Garden of Victory; Let Us Adorn Our Country with Gardens

THE FOREST: In the Forest (*by Ivan Turgenev*); The Forest Glade; How Trees Move (*by Leo Tolstoy*); Why Forests Are Valuable; The Forest of the Future (*poem*); Beetles; The Forest Drummer (*woodpecker*); The Green Apothecary Shop; Following Tracks; A Squirrel Hunt

FORMS OF THE EARTH'S SURFACE: The Black Earth Plains; On a Mountain Top; Along a Mountain Path in the Caucasus; Iron, Steel, and Pen Knives

WATER IN NATURE: How River Are Formed; The Source of the Volga; Ravines; Fortifying Ravines; The Moscow Canal; Our Volga; The Terek (*by Mikhail Lermontov*); A Hurricane at Sea

INHABITANTS OF THE WATER: In the Lake; The Whale; Hunting Whales; On the Antarctic Ice

AMPHIBIANS AND SNAKES: The Metamorphosis of Frogs; The Grass Snake and the Adder

CLIMATE: Why Do We Have Wind? (*by Leo Tolstoy*); During a Storm (*by Ivan Goncharov*); The Barometer; Who Needs to Know the Weather and Why; What Is Climate?

THE HUMAN BODY: The Skeleton; The Skeleton of Men and Horses; The Spine; Curvature of the Spine; The Rib Cage; Muscles; The Work of Muscles; Muscles Develop with Use; Food; Where Food Goes when We Eat; How to Take Care of Your Teeth; Vitamins; Contagious Diseases; Microbes; How Contagious Diseases Are Communicated; The Lungs; The Skin; The Circulation of the Blood; The Heart; What to Do If You Cut Your Finger; The Organs of Sense; Sight; How Our Eyes Are Protected from Many Dangers; Hearing; Taste; The Sense of Smell; The Sense of Touch

GREAT RUSSIAN INVENTORS AND EXPLORERS:   Ivan Polzunov (*inventor*); The Russian Inventor Ivan Kulibin; The Great Russian Inventor Alexander Popov; Maklai among the Papuans; Nicholas Przhyevalsky (*explorer*)

### III.   HISTORY SECTION

FROM OUR COUNTRY'S PAST:   How the Slavs Lived; Alexander Nevsky; The Tatar Invasion of Russia; The Founding of Moscow; Our Ancient Capital (*poem*); Moscow; On the Field of Kulikovo; Minin and Pozharsky; The War with the Swedes; The Founding of Petersburg; The Battle of Poltava (*poem by Alexander Pushkin*); General Suvorov; The Capture of Izmail; The War of 1812; The Bold Sailor; The Unreaped Field (*poem by Nicholas Nekrassov*); The Struggle of the Peasants Against the Landowners; A Revolutionary Song; Nicholas Petrovitch; Bloody Sunday; The Overthrow of the Autocracy

FROM THE HISTORY OF OUR SOCIALIST COUNTRY:   Storming the Winter Palace; Civil War; Voroshilov at the Front; From the Life of Nicholas Shchors; Chapayev in Battle; The Death of Chapayev; The Brave Partisan; Gregory Kotovsky; A Trip to Kashino; In the Lenin Museum (*poem*)

THE FIVE-YEAR PLANS:   The First Five-Year Plan; The Second Five-Year Plan; A New River; Machine-Tractor Stations; A Birthplace

THE SECOND WORLD WAR:   To A Noble People (*poem*); Stalingrad; A Song about Stalingrad; The Story of a Tank Driver; The Nightingale (*a war story*)

POSTWAR RECONSTRUCTION:   Lenin Is With Us (*poem*); The Five-Year Plan; Our Glorious Homeland (*poem*); How Man Uses Rivers

# Fourth-Grade Soviet Reader

*Title:* RODNAYA RECH (Native Language)
*Vocabulary:* Approximately 10,000 words

## CONTENTS

*(Pre-Soviet authors are given in parentheses)*

### INTRODUCTION

A Word About Our Mother Country; Our Native Land; Be Prepared for the Struggle in the Cause of the Communist Party

### SUMMER

Welcome, Young Travelers; The Happy Tourist; Grandfather Tyeryoshkin; The Pioneer Campfire; Night; Hunting the Hawk; How to Get over Groundless Fears (*by Alexander Herzen*); The Peasant's Children (*by Nicholas Nekrassov*); Nekrassov's Childhood; A Woman's Lot (*by Nicholas Nekrassov*); On the Volga (*by Nicholas Nekrassov*); A Summer Fire; Rye (*poem*); The Steppes

### AUTUMN

Autumn (*by Alexander Pushkin*); An Autumn Day in the Woods (*by Ivan Turgenev*); The Cranes Fly (*by Ivan Turgenev*); The Traveling Frog (*by Vselovod Mikhailovitch Garshin*)

### FAIRY TALES, LEGENDS, FABLES

The Green Oak (*by Alexander Pushkin*); From the Life of Pushkin; The Fairy Tale of the Czar-Saltan (*15-page poem by Alexander Pushkin*); Ruslan and Liudmila (*mock-epic poem*

48

# Fourth-Grade American Reader

*Title:* *Singing Wheels*
*Series:* THE ALICE AND JERRY BASIC READING PROGRAM
*Publisher:* Row, Peterson and Company
*Author:* Mabel O'Donnell

*From "Word List" (printed in the back of the book)*

". . . includes 532 words . . . that were not taught in the preceding
books of the ALICE AND JERRY BASIC READING PROGRAM"

## CONTENTS

*(All selections are unsigned and are thus presumably written
by the author)*

*by Alexander Pushkin*); The Blue Carpet (*Tajik legend*); The Hot Stone; A Song about a Pioneer's Dream; Two Dogs (*by Ivan Krylov*); The Cuckoo and the Cock (*fable by Ivan Krylov*); The Fox and the Crow (*fable by Ivan Krylov*); The Peasant and the Worker (*fable by Ivan Krylov*)

### THE FAMILY, STORIES ABOUT CHILDREN

A Mother's Love; In a New Family; The Big Birch; Vanka (*by Anton Chekhov*); How Gorky Read Books (*by Maxim Gorky*); The Sparrow (*by Ivan Turgenev*); True Friends; My Friend; What Shall I Be?; Friendship (*by Vladimir Korolenko*); Karagoz (*by Mikhail Lermontov*); Mumu (*by Ivan Turgenev*); Vanya the Shepherd Boy; A March (*by Nicholas Nekrassov*); In a Gymnasium; Gavrosh; The Drummers' Plot

### WINTER

The Biting Frost (*by Alexander Pushkin*); Winter (*by Alexander Pushkin*); A Winter Morning (*by Alexander Pushkin*); Winter; A Winter in Studyony (*by Dimitri Mamin-Sibiryak*); A Night in the Forest; Conquering the Taiga

### SPRING

Spring (*by Alexander Pushkin*); In the Spring (*by Anton Chekhov*); Spring; The Opening of the River; Moscow in May

### FROM OUR COUNTRY'S PAST

On the Seashore (*by Alexander Pushkin*); Mikhail Lomonosov (*biography*); General Suvorov (*biography*); Grandfather (*by Nicholas Nekrassov*); The Caucasian Prisoner (*by Leo Tolstoy*); Ilya Efimovitch Repin (*biography*); The Rooks Have Flown Away; The First of May (*by Maxim Gorky*)

THE PEOPLE OF THE SOVIET COUNTRIES

Lenin Goes to Smolny; In Smolny; The Seizure of the Telephone Station; A Wealthy Man; We Are Thirty Years Old; Tanya; The Young Guard (*selection from a Soviet novel*); A Story of a Son; The Will to Live; The Last Day of Matvey Kuxmin; I Am Always Living; According to Lenin's Plan; Visions; We Need Peace; Glory to the People (*poem*)

# 2

## LITERATURE
## IN SOVIET AND AMERICAN
## SCHOOLS

A sound literary education is of inestimable value to students, for not only does a close acquaintance with important literary works increase immeasurably the student's ability to understand and enjoy and use his language, but it provides emotional and aesthetic and intellectual experiences which contribute to his taste, his judgment, and his maturity in a way that no other subject can. We may well ask how great a contribution to a student's education American textbooks make as compared to Soviet textbooks.

### LITERATURE IN THE FIFTH AND
### SIXTH GRADES IN RUSSIAN
### AND AMERICAN SCHOOLS

Although a fairly large proportion of the selections in the RODNAYA RECH readers are from the works of the best Russian authors, there is no attempt, of course, in these early grades to introduce a formal study of literature. The chief aim of these texts is to teach Soviet students to read well enough so that by the time they reach the fifth grade they can begin their formal study of literature, which in fact they do.

The syllabus used in Soviet schools for the teaching of literature provides a useful description of the aims of the literary program for the fifth and sixth grades.

Students in the fifth grade receive an elementary understanding of the literature of Russian folklore and some of its categories (fairy tales, proverbs, and riddles). By analyzing literary works students learn to find the basic idea expressed in the work and become acquainted with the peculiarities of its construction. In the fifth grade the students are given a general understanding of narration and description. They also master an understanding of the pictorial qualities of language in artistic works (the epithet, the simile, the metaphor, and personification), and they receive an elementary notion of the distinction between artistic and non-artistic language.

In the sixth grade this elementary understanding of literary theory is expanded and extended. Students become acquainted with the peculiarities of the structure and language of folk literature (stories and folk songs). They are given an understanding of the themes and ideas of literary works. From these elementary observations about the structure of literary works, students of the sixth grade proceed to a thorough understanding of the basic kinds of expression in literary works: of narration, description, characterization, dialogue, and also of the kinds of description (portraits, landscapes, descriptions of objects, and of situations). From a general notion of the poetry and prose of language, the sixth-grade student proceeds to an acquaintance with the qualities of poetry (an understanding of poetic rhythm, two and three syllable feet, accent, and rhyme). Finally, in the sixth grade, students acquire an understanding of the epic and the lyric poem and master the important forms of narrative works (the tale, the story, the fable).

—*Programmi srednei scholi, Russky yazik i
literaturnie chtenie, v-vii klassi*
(Programs of the middle schools, Russian
language and literature, grades 5-7), pp. 23-24.

The contents of the Soviet fifth- and sixth-grade literature texts clearly reflect these aims. A glance at the table of contents of the Soviet fifth-grade literature book, which is no longer called RODNAYA RECH (Native Language) but RODNAYA LITERATURA (Native Literature) will show that it is divided into three main parts. (See the table of contents at the end of this chapter.) It consists of (1) selections from Russian folklore tradition; (2) selections from Russian writers of the past; and (3) selections by Soviet writers. Of the 220 pages in this book, all but 25 pages are devoted to pre-Soviet literature, and 175 pages consist of poems, stories, tales, and fables by Pushkin, Turgenev, Krylov, Shevchenko, Goncharov, Nekrassov, Leo Tolstoy, Chekhov, Korolenko, and Gorky. In addition there are one- or two-page discussions of such literary genres as the tale, the fable, and the poem, and of such literary techniques and devices as narration, description, dialogue, the epithet, and the simile. There are also biographical essays, averaging 9 pages in length, of Pushkin, Turgenev, and Shevchenko. The longer selections include Turgenev's 26-page story "Mumu," a 16-page excerpt from Goncharov's novel *Oblomov,* and an 18-page tale by Chekhov called "Kashtanka." *All of these selections are reproduced unaltered and unabridged from the originals.*

The sixth-grade literature book used in the Soviet schools is devoted entirely to Russian literature before 1900. (See the table of contents at the end of this chapter.) It is divided into two main parts. The first is a short collection (31 pages) of early Russian tales, stories, and poems, including two- or three-page discussions of Russian popular epic poems, popular folk heroes, poetical peculiarities of Russian popular epic poems, and the characteristics of folk songs. The second and much longer part (225 text pages, without illustrations), consists of selections from the works of five major Russian writers: Krylov, Pushkin, Lermontov, Gogol, and Turgenev.

These selections are preceded by a biographical sketch of

each author, ranging from 2 pages (Gogol) to 10 pages (Pushkin). In addition, each selection is followed by a commentary, sometimes running to 5 or 6 pages, on each selection. The longer works include Pushkin's 60-page story *Dybrovsky* in its entirety, and 55 pages of Gogol's *Taras Bulba*.

While the fifth- and sixth-grade literature program in Soviet schools is thus in orbit, the literature program for the same grades in American schools is fizzling on the launching pad. The quality of the fifth- and sixth-grade books of the typical American basal reader series shows no radical improvement over the quality of the readers of the earlier grades. But the vocabulary in most of them does expand at a somewhat faster rate than in the earlier grades. The fifth-grade reader is likely to have a vocabulary of 2,000 or 2,500 words, and the sixth-grade reader a vocabulary of as many as 4,000 words, though a number of readers have closer to 3,000 words—a smaller vocabulary than is contained in the second-grade RODNAYA RECH reader.

Some of these American readers do loosen their vocabulary-control apparatus in the fifth and sixth grades by merely including a glossary of hard words in the back of the book, but many others follow the same procedure as the earlier books of introducing only a few words on each page—now sometimes as many as six—and of repeating the words from time to time.

There is also some improvement in the choice of reading selections for the fifth- and sixth-grade readers, but in general, while fifth-grade Soviet students are reading Pushkin and Tolstoy and Chekhov in quantity, American students are still reading very much the same insipid stuff which fills their earlier readers.

The fifth-grade book in the NEW BASIC READING PROGRAM, for example, has a few children's selections by Kipling and Aesop and A. A. Milne and Dr. Seuss, along with some Indian, Greek, and Arabian tales, which, together with 82 pages of accounts of a rather odd assortment of distinguished people, make up a third of the book; but the other two-thirds has no literary value whatsoever. The fifth-grade book in the GINN BASIC READERS series sports poems by Stephen Vincent Benét, Longfellow, Rachel Field, James Russell Lowell, and Edward Lear as well as four pages of *The Peterkin Papers* and some legends about Pandora, Thor, Robin Hood, King Arthur, and William Tell, but nothing else that is worth mentioning. The fifth-grade book in the EASY GROWTH READING SERIES has nothing more literary than a selection from Eric Knight's *Lassie Come Home*, and the fifth-grade reader in the ALICE AND JERRY books has nothing of any literary value whatsoever. The reader may wish to inspect the table of contents of a typical fifth-grade reader, which has been reprinted at the end of this chapter.

And while sixth-grade Soviet students are steeped in the high-powered Russian literature of the nineteenth century, their American counterparts are getting pretty low-voltage stuff. The only impressive selections in the reader for the first half of the sixth grade in the NEW BASIC READING PROGRAM are 9 pages of *Dr. Doolittle,* 15 pages of Robert Lawson's *Ben and Me,* and a poem by Rachel Field. Winston's sixth-grade reader in the EASY GROWTH IN READING SERIES has only four recognizable literary works, all poems, and one of them a nonsense poem. Students who read the sixth-grade book in the GINN BASIC READERS series fare a little better. They read 7 lines of Shakespeare; poems by Leigh Hunt, Lewis Carroll, and Hamlin Garland; stories by Cornelia Meigs and Dorothy Canfield; and 35 pages of stories about the Trojan Horse, Demeter and Persephone, David and Goliath, and the Sorcerer's Apprentice. But these selections make up only 12 to 14 per cent of the book. The DEVELOPMENTAL READING PROGRAM reader for the sixth grade, which boasts a total vocabulary of 3,226 words and which is called *Stories to Remember,* has only one selection which has ever been remembered, namely Masefield's "Sea Fever." Houghton Mifflin's sixth-grade reader, which has "876 new words," has a poem apiece by Sara Teasdale, Dr. Seuss,

Carl Sandburg, Robert Frost, Arthur Guiterman, and a story by Andrew Lang in adapted form, all mixed in with a vast amount of wretched writing. The sixth-grade reader in the ALICE AND JERRY books still has absolutely nothing of literary merit. The table of contents of a typical sixth-grade reader is printed at ,the end of this chapter.

It will be evident, I think, that I have given the widest possible interpretation to the word *literary* in assessing the literary value of these selections, inasmuch as many of even the best of them are only on the fringes of literature, and of these, several are selections by children's authors. And there are of course no discussions of literary works or literary theory, because these books have so few literary works to discuss or to theorize about.

One can thus conclude that the contribution which the typical fifth- and sixth-grade American readers make to our children's literary education is negligible, and that the contribution that the fifth- and sixth-grade Soviet literature textbooks make to the literary education of Soviet students is impressive.

## RUSSIAN LITERATURE TEXTBOOKS IN THE SEVENTH THROUGH TENTH GRADES

There are fewer selections in the seventh-grade Soviet literature book, which is still called RODNAYA LITERATURA (Native Literature), than in the one for the sixth grade. A large part of the book is devoted to the works of Soviet writers, though some of the best Soviet writers are represented, namely, Gorky, Mayakovsky, and Nicholas Ostrovsky. However, the first part of the book is assigned to nineteenth-century Russian writers and includes selections from Nekrassov, Leo Tolstoy, and Chekhov, followed by short discussions of literary types, humor, and satire, and a brief essay on the significance of Russian literature. (See the table of contents at the end of this chapter.) But despite the mature style of the selections and the rather sophisticated discussion of literary terms, the seventh-grade literature book on the whole offers less-distinguished selections than the ones in later grades.

The literature anthologies for the eighth, ninth, and tenth grades mark the final stage of the literary program in Russian schools—a detailed survey of Russian literature from its origins to the present time. The books are supplemented by three other volumes, which present a similarly detailed study of the history of Russian literature as well as considerable training in literary theory and criticism.

This stage of the program begins in the eighth grade with an enormous anthology of 660 pictureless pages called RUSSKAYA LITERATURA (Russian Literature), which consists entirely of Russian literature written before 1850. (See the end of this chapter for the table of contents to this book.) It is divided into three parts, as follows: (1) literature of ancient Russia (28 pages); (2) literature of the eighteenth century (42 pages); and (3) literature of the nineteenth century (580 pages). The first part includes excerpts from early chronicles and epic poems; the second consists of selections by eighteenth-century Russian writers, including Lomonosov, Derzhavin, Fonvizin, Radishchev, and Karamzin. The third and much longer part includes from among the works of Pushkin, 19 poems, one short play and *Boris Godunov* (condensed), *Eugene Onegin* (his famous novel in verse, slightly condensed), and his novel *The Captain's Daughter* (complete). Lermontov's *A Hero of Our Time* (abridged) is also included, as well as Gogol's *Dead Souls* (abridged) and his play *The Inspector General* (complete); finally there appear a large number of articles and letters from the works of the nineteenth-century critic Vissarion Belinsky.

But studying this imposing array of masterpieces of Russia's greatest writers does not constitute all the literary training that

Soviet students receive in the eighth grade. They are also supplied with a 300-page companion volume to the large anthology. This book, also called RUSSKAYA LITERATURA, is in fact a history of Russian literature from its origins to 1850. It consists of detailed and thoroughly adult discussions of the authors, periods, literary movements, influences, and major literary works that make up Russian literary history. Each chapter is followed by questions, and students are expected to master all the material in the book.

The ninth-grade literature program continues the approach of that of the eighth grade, but the readings cover only the last half of nineteenth-century Russian literature and some foreign classics from various periods. They include selections from Goncharov's novel *Oblomov,* Alexander Ostrovsky's play *The Thunderstorm,* chapters from Chernyshevsky's *What Is to Be Done?,* some poems by Nekrassov, some tales by Saltykov, Tolstoy's *War and Peace* in its entirety, Chekhov's *The Cherry Orchard,* Shakespeare's *Hamlet,* and Goethe's *Faust,* Part I. These readings are similarly accompanied by a 340-page book which discusses in detail the main literary movements, the chief Russian writers, and the most important works between the years 1850 and 1900. (See the table of contents at the end of this chapter.)

The literature program for the tenth grade continues this detailed study of Russian literature and concentrates on the literature of the twentieth century. The text includes the play *The Lower Depths* (condensed) and 80 pages from the novel *Mother* from the works of Gorky, some poems by Mayakovsky, excerpts from Nicholas Ostrovsky's novel *The Tempering of the Steel,* from Sholokhov's novel *The Virgin Soil Upturned,* and from Fadeyev's novel *The Young Guard,* and some selections from non-Russian Soviet writers. All this is supplemented by a 400-page companion volume which is a detailed history of Russian literature in the twentieth century.

It seems evident from this program that by the time the

Soviet student finishes the tenth grade he has been fairly thoroughly exposed to the literature of his language. Both the quantity and the quality are impressive, and it should perhaps be re-emphasized that the majority of the selections in these anthologies are pre-Soviet, and that many of them are by authors who are widely read in our own country. For ideological reasons, the only major pre-Soviet writer not represented at all in these anthologies is Dostoyevsky, but several pages in the ninth-grade literature text are devoted to a discussion of his life and works—referring to him as "a famous Russian writer"—and his novels *Poor Folk, The Insulted and the Injured,* and *Memoirs from a Dead House* are on the list of recommended outside reading, though none of his later and more important works are so recommended.

But the quantity and quality of the readings are not the only impressive features of the literary program in the Soviet schools; equally impressive is the thorough training Soviet students receive in the history of Russian literature, in biographical knowledge of the authors, and in literary history and literary theory —training which, as I have indicated, begins in the fifth grade and continues through the tenth. How far this literary theory and literary criticism are distorted to serve Communist ends I shall suggest in the concluding chapter of this study. I wish here only to point out that the theory and criticism are thorough and detailed. The thoroughness with which the literary works themselves are studied may be suggested by the fact that in the ninth grade, teachers are instructed to spend fourteen class periods on Turgenev's *Fathers and Sons* and twenty-eight hours on Tolstoy's *War and Peace.*

## LITERATURE IN THE SEVENTH THROUGH NINTH GRADES IN AMERICAN SCHOOLS

The readers and anthologies used in the junior high schools in the United States constitute a kind of literary limbo. There is very little good literature in them, some mediocre literature, and a great deal that is not literature at all.

By and large, the literature textbooks used in these grades are not literature anthologies at all, but readers from which students are still learning to read. The distinction between the approach and purpose of a reader and a literature anthology can be seen by a quick glance at the contents. If the contents are arranged according to author or according to types of literature, e.g., poems, short stories, plays, novels, and so forth, or according to chronological periods, i.e., by centuries or other commonly designated periods, then the book attempts to be a genuine literary anthology. On the other hand, if the selections are arranged according to subject or general topic— such as our animal friends, stories of adventure, people to remember, and so on—then it is not a literature anthology but a reader.

This distinction is important because the selections in the readers in the junior high schools are usually quite inferior in quality to the selections in a genuine literature anthology. When selections in a reader are grouped around general subjects, the overwhelming tendency among editors is to find pieces which fit in with the general topic, and if they come out of an old copy of *Boys' Life* or the most recent story in a popular magazine, so much the better; or if a piece happens to be written by an established author, it is commonly among his lesser works because his best works do not fit into the general scheme of the book. The tables of contents of both the

Soviet and the American readers and anthologies printed at the end of this chapter illustrate this phenomenon.

The readers and anthologies most commonly used in our junior high schools are also published in series, like those of the lower grades. The worst of them, generally speaking, are the seventh- and eighth-grade readers that are continuations of the reader series for the first six grades, such as the seventh- and eighth-grade readers of the GINN BASIC READERS series, the NEW BASIC READING PROGRAM (Scott, Foresman), the READING FOR MEANING PROGRAM, the MACMILLAN READERS SERIES, or the SHELDON BASIC READING SERIES (Allyn and Bacon). Readers of this sort merely continue the practice of the earlier books in the series of avoiding selections that are either very difficult or very good. But the literary value of the selections is nearly as limited in the early volumes of such high school series as the ADVENTURES IN LITERATURE PROGRAM (Harcourt, Brace), the LITERATURE AND LIFE SERIES (Scott, Foresman), the PROSE AND POETRY SERIES (Singer), the AMERICA READS SERIES (Scott, Foresman), the READING FOR LIFE SERIES (Lippincott) or the READING LITERATURE SERIES (Row, Peterson).

The newest and in most cases the most widely used series are strongly influenced by the educational philosophy which holds that students should learn about the minutiae of daily living on school time. Most of these readers, for example, have a section on sports. The titles of a few of the selections suggest well enough what students read under this heading: "Pass That Puck!" "Lou Gehrig Joins the Yankees," "Fast Ball" by Bob Feller, and "Baseball and Books" by Wally Moon, which consists of 6 pages with 14 illustrations of Moon and the Cardinals in action and a rundown of Moon's batting average over a three-year period.

Most of these readers also have a section of humorous stories and poems which may go under some such title as "For the Fun of It" or "Laughing Together." But many of the selections here do not rise much about the limerick level or the "Private

Zoo" level of Ogden Nash, and some are proudly nonsensical. Many third graders are quite capable of understanding and fully appreciating the majority of selections which appear under this head in a junior high reader.

Sometimes the headings themselves are utterly inane, as for example, "Here We Are" or "It Might Happen to You," and under them can be and generally are grouped selections that can and do illustrate almost anything—except good literature.

There are usually sections, too, which treat various aspects of American history, biography, and science, and though the informational value of some of the selections is considerable and even though some are written by recognizable authors, the over-all literary quality of these is unimpressive, to say the least. At any rate rarely are the biographies by or about the most noteworthy men, or the history selections about the most important events, or the science section about the great landmarks of scientific discovery. The biography section of one ninth-grade literature book, for example, does have ten chapters from Sandburg's *Abe Lincoln Grows Up*, but also included are such selections as "My Papa" by Lloyd C. Douglas, "My Grandmother and Her Many Harbors" by Mary Ellen Chase, "The Thread That Runs So True," by Jesse Stuart, "Son of the South," by Rackham Holt, and "A Dishwasher Addresses Rotary," by Salom Rizk. None of these last selections are wholly valueless, though in the light of the biographical classics the book might have included, they are very nearly so.

I wish now to dispel any impression I may have created that there is nothing of literary value in these junior high school textbooks. In the poetry selections, for example, there are such poets as Phyllis McGinley, Ogden Nash, Rosemary and Stephen Vincent Benét, Cornelia Meigs, Robert Frost, Sara Teasdale, Jesse Stuart, Carl Sandburg, John Greenleaf Whittier, Eugene Field, Vachel Lindsay, and Henry Wadsworth Longfellow among others, but many are much less well known or virtually unknown.

In the matter of short stories, there are, of course, some stories by established authors, such as Jack London, Bret Harte, O. Henry, James Thurber, and Edgar Allan Poe, and even Maupassant, but again the largest percentage are by unimportant authors whom even the most widely read persons will find totally unfamiliar.

However, the drama section in these readers—if there is one —is almost always highly suspect. Here the educational theory that students must be kept abreast of the most recent developments of life around them has exerted a strong influence. The customary practice is to include texts or librettos or scripts of plays or musical comedies which have had a recent success— the more recent the better—on Broadway or on television or radio. The drama section of one highly popular ninth-grade junior high school literature book, for example, consists of the following: a one-act play called *The Stolen Prince* by Dan Totheroh, a radio play called *Never Come Monday* by Eric Knight and Stephen Fox, a one-act play called *The Valiant* by Holworthy Hall and Robert Middlemass, and a television play called *The Dancers* by Horton Foote.

The English novel, if one is included, is usually the high point of the typical ninth-grade reader or anthology, though the novel may be abridged.

One particularly interesting phenomenon sometimes observable in these readers and anthologies is the inclusion of selections from the works of America's best authors, but presented not in their original form but in some other and modernized form. Thus one eighth-grade book has Oliver Wendell Holmes' poem "The Deacon's Masterpiece" adapted for radio in the form of a dialogue between a "Narrator" and a "Stooge"; another eighth-grade reader presents the whitewashing scene in *Tom Sawyer* as a television play, with nearly as many words of stage directions as of dialogue.

In examining these readers and anthologies one naturally asks the question: to what extent are America's finest authors represented? Where, for example, are appropriate selections from the works of Nathaniel Hawthorne, Herman Melville, Henry David Thoreau, Washington Irving, Ralph Waldo Emerson, James Fenimore Cooper, Edith Wharton, Mark Twain, Edwin Arlington Robinson, Benjamin Franklin, Thomas Jefferson, Francis Parkman, and so on. It would be a mistake indeed to say that none of these authors are presented in our junior high school literature books, but it is no mistake to say that in any given book most of them are not represented and that those who are represented are usually poorly represented.

One may well ask, too, how well English authors are represented in these literature textbooks. Since the English people speak and write a language not unlike our own and since their literature has achieved a certain degree of distinction, one might expect to find English literature well represented in these textbooks. But again, though one cannot say that it is entirely neglected in them, it is almost neglected, or if not neglected, then badly represented.

By the same token it should be observed that a junior high literature book is rare indeed if more than 5 per cent of its selections were written before 1800, or if more than 30 per cent were written before 1900. The emphasis is overwhelmingly upon twentieth-century authors, and unfortunately upon the relatively unimportant ones.

But there is yet another important feature of the typical junior high school literature textbook which speaks against it. The rank childishness of the readers used in the elementary schools makes it seem necessary for many of the editors and publishers of junior high literature textbooks to do everything but stand on their heads in order to entice the student to read the words that are in the text, if not to enjoy them. Not only are the covers of these books colorful, but the books themselves contain many illustrations, often in color, and many photographs, drawings, and even cartoons, so that often every other page is decorated with a picture of some sort, and the print in most of these books is very large. In one book, the introduction is written by Mary Martin and the text of the introduction is interspersed with 19 illustrations (7 in color) of Mary Martin as she appears at home and on the set of a performance of *Peter Pan*.

As a result of shenanigans of this sort, one cannot help being struck with the immaturity of many of the junior high literature texts now on the market. It can be said in defense of them that even if they don't contain much literature, they are at least pretty to look at, and indeed some of them are very pretty to look at. It would seem, however, that the very aesthetic features of the format of these books in fact work against the student, for it is as if there were a desperate attempt to make the written word seem palatable, as if the enjoyment of the pictures were a reward for the rather nasty job of reading the words. The net effect, however, may well be that the student turns the page not to see what the next page says but what the next picture looks like. At any rate, insofar as the colorful and funny illustrations have the effect of drawing attention away from the printed words, they ill prepare a student, psychologically and actually, to cope with good books, the vast majority of which have no pictures, colored or otherwise, and in which the print is rarely anything but normal-sized. The transition from the newest junior high school literature textbooks to the abundance of good literature available in paperback form, for example, is a transition so formidable that students may prefer to avoid making it.

Everyone, of course, welcomes a book with a handsome format, but in the matter of textbooks it is well to select those which will *contribute* to a student's maturity rather than *retard* it. Yet, the trend seems to be that the newer the junior high literature textbook is, the prettier it looks, the more colored pictures it has, the larger the print, the fewer the words, and the less literary the selections. One eighth-grade reader has a selection entitled "Telling a Favorite Story in a New Way."

The selection turns out to be a story told in pictures and captions of how another story is told on TV. At the present rate, this may be a hint of what the junior high literature textbook of the future will be like. But even the typical junior high literature textbook of the present, it must be concluded, does precious little to acquaint our children with their literary heritage.

## LITERATURE IN AMERICAN HIGH SCHOOLS

Even as late as the tenth grade, our students are not likely to learn very much about literature from their textbooks. Few of the books are organized around authors or around literary periods, though they are often organized around literary types. These observations are corroborated by a publication of the U. S. Office of Education reporting on a survey of 285 courses of study in 44 states. This report points out that "approximately 60 per cent of the local courses of study containing unit topics suggest that some or all literature in grade 10 be organized and taught by literary type. Eighteen per cent of all local courses recommend that the thematic or idea-centered unit predominate. The remaining 22 per cent suggest one or more types of organization: Author, literary period, or chronological development." (Arno Jewett, *English Language Arts in American High Schools*. U. S. Department of Health, Education, and Welfare. Office of Education. Bulletin 1958, No. 13, p. 65.)

One of the important differences between the Soviet and American literature programs in the tenth grade is that the Soviet student is exposed to a systematic presentation of the major Soviet authors, whereas the American tenth grader reads a scattering of stories, poems, plays, and novels from various periods, making the systematic study of literature impossible. Students may or may not enjoy reading a play by Shakespeare or a novel by George Eliot in the tenth grade, but, unless their teachers are extraordinarily talented, they will learn little from such a hodgepodge about either Elizabethan drama or the Victorian novel on the one hand or Shakespeare or George Eliot on the other. In this connection the U. S. Office of Education publication referred to above further states that "as in the junior high school, few classics are prescribed for study in grade 10," and it goes on to point out that the notable exceptions are *Julius Caesar, Silas Marner,* and *A Tale of Two Cities,* the first of which is required in the tenth grade by about half the local courses of study. All in all, however, the literature program of the first year of high school is commonly not auspicious, at least in those classes which use the typical tenth-grade English anthology. (See the table of contents at the end of this chapter.)

Until the new eleven-year school program gets underway in the Soviet Union, most Soviet students, especially those in the cities, end their formal schooling with the tenth grade.* But, as we have seen, they leave school with a pretty thorough awareness of the literature written in the Russian language. Hundreds of thousands of our students leave school at the end of the twelfth grade, after having been in school for two years longer than Soviet students, but our students' textbooks—particularly through the tenth grade—have given them very little cumulative knowledge of the literature written in the English language.

It is true that in the eleventh grade of most high schools our children are finally introduced to the serious study of literature —but it is the classic example of too little, too late. Approximately 80 per cent of the students in the eleventh grade study American literature, usually based on a chronological approach. Here for the first time they become acquainted with some of the best American authors and learn about literary movements and literary periods, and they often learn from as

* See Appendix B.

good textbooks as could be expected for a survey course.

It is by no means certain, however, that they will continue their literary education in the twelfth grade. The publication referred to above, for example, states that "in grade 12, the traditionally required course in English literature, organized on a chronological basis, seems to be slowly losing ground." It reports that fewer than half the local courses of study have a required course in English literature, though 12 per cent offer it in the eleventh grade. World literature fares even worse than English literature in American high schools, for it is required in the twelfth grade in only 13 per cent of the local courses of study which specify programs in literature, and by a negligible number in the earlier grades. Thus, the chances that a student will get courses in American literature *and* English literature *and* world literature are slight, and he has less than an even chance of getting any two of these courses.

But even if he were to take both American literature and English literature survey courses, our curriculum compares very unfavorably with that of Soviet schools. It will be observed, for example, that whereas Soviet students spend three years in a detailed study of Russian literature presented chronologically in the eighth, ninth, and tenth grades, our students try to cover comparable ground in one year. The quick survey of American literature from Captain John Smith to H. Allen Smith, and the similar twelfth-grade survey of English literature from Beowulf to Virginia Woolf, is bound to leave them bewildered. It even leaves college sophomores bewildered.

Some readings in the eleventh- and twelfth-grade survey courses no doubt make vivid and lasting impressions on some students, and good teachers in these grades are able to give some students a lasting love for literature and a genuine understanding of it. But about all that most high school seniors are likely to have left at the end of these two survey courses is a jumbled recollection of names and titles and snatches of poems and bits of prose. They are just as likely to come away from their American-literature survey course thinking that Henry James wrote *The Scarlet Letter* aboard the *Mayflower* as they are to come away from their English-literature course thinking that Samuel Johnson was a famous nineteenth-century Elizabethan playwright. English professors know that I am not exaggerating.

It will be seen, then, that the contrasts in the degree of thoroughness between the literature programs in Soviet and American schools are rather sharp. The lack of depth in the teaching of literature in our schools may perhaps be most dramatically illustrated by a description of how much more thoroughly Soviet students study major authors than American students do. In their study of Tolstoy, for example, Soviet students read 7 selections by him in the first grade, 8 in the second, 5 in the third, and one in the fourth. In the literature anthologies of the later grades, they read one selection in the fifth, and one in the seventh: a chapter of *War and Peace.* In the ninth they read virtually the entire novel *War and Peace,* and in addition they read a 55-page commentary on Tolstoy's life and works in their history-of-Russian-literature text.

Soviet students read even more by and about Pushkin. Ten of his poems are in the readers of the first three grades, and 9 are in their fourth-grade reader. In the literature anthologies and histories of the later grades, they read 30 pages of Pushkin's life, his poems, his stories, and commentaries on his works in the fifth grade, more than 80 pages of his works in the sixth grade, and 220 pages in the eighth grade, including 19 poems, 2 plays, his verse novel *Eugene Onegin,* and his novel *The Captain's Daughter.* All this is in addition to 80 pages of biographical and critical material on Pushkin which appears in the textbook on the history of Russian literature for the eighth grade.

The thoroughness with which Soviet students study other major pre-Soviet Russian authors can be similarly demonstrated by reference to the selections and the biographical and critical commentaries in Soviet textbooks on Gogol, Turgenev, Chekhov, Krylov, Belinsky, Goncharov, Lomonosov, and others.

This study of major pre-Soviet Russian authors which begins as early as the first grade and continues almost uninterruptedly through the eighth or ninth grade involves not only wide reading in the works of these authors, but considerable biographical and critical commentary, so that over a period of eight or nine years, the literature as well as the lives of major pre-Soviet Russian writers is bound to make an indelible impression on the minds of even the most mediocre students, and this knowledge and literary experience thus become an important part of the Soviet student's education.

American textbooks, on the other hand, give our students nothing comparable in thoroughness and depth in their study of American authors. Educators and scholars would no doubt find great difficulty in agreeing on the ten or twelve greatest American authors, but perhaps among twenty or thirty of the greatest, most of them would include Nathaniel Hawthorne, James Fenimore Cooper, Ralph Waldo Emerson, Washington Irving, Emily Dickinson, Herman Melville, Henry James, Walt Whitman, Edgar Allan Poe, Mark Twain, and Henry David Thoreau. At what grade, then, do our children read these authors or at least read about them in their textbooks? As I have indicated, the nature of their readers in the elementary grades precludes their reading anything at all by them unless by chance a poem or two by Emily Dickinson has been inserted surreptitiously. The nature of the typical junior high school reader also places strong odds against students' reading much of the works of these authors, though it is not impossible that some Poe or a chapter of *Tom Sawyer* may be in their reader, or perhaps a radio script of *The Legend of Sleepy Hollow*. Nor can one by any means safely assume that tenth-grade literature textbooks will represent any of these authors. Students can, it is true, be fairly certain of reading snatches from the works of most of these authors in the eleventh grade, but only along with the works of twenty or thirty lesser authors with whom they might easily be confused.

If major American literary works and authors are badly represented in textbooks for the first ten grades, it seems unnecessary to observe that major English works and authors are even more poorly represented. In fact, except for the English novel and the Shakespearian play that usually appear in the tenth-grade anthologies and except for some isolated poems by nineteenth- and twentieth-century English poets, English literature in most readers and literature anthologies before the twelfth grade is slightly regarded.

It is interesting to note too that Soviet literature books devote a good deal of space to the biographies of famous Russian writers, even as early as the fifth and sixth grades. These writers are advanced as heroes of a sort and are offered as objects of admiration if not emulation. Any Soviet student who has mastered the biographical information which these literature textbooks offer knows a great deal indeed about Russian authors, though it must be admitted that this information often creates a false impression of the author's life.

American readers and literature books, on the other hand, commonly devote little attention to the lives of famous American authors. One reason for this, of course, is that, as we have seen, the works of most of our best authors are not represented in the readers and anthologies before the eleventh grade. And sometimes it is as if the editors of American textbooks were trying to hide the very existence of our authors. Some readers, for example, do not even print the names of such authors as Robert Frost, Carl Sandburg, and Sara Teasdale opposite the name of their selections in the book, but mention them only in the Acknowledgments. And in many, if not most, readers at the junior high level such biographical information about authors as may be supplied is often simply a squib, with no emphasis on distinguished authors.

Fortunately, in their grade school and high school years some American students do a considerable amount of outside reading. How much of this outside reading is assigned or encouraged by the schools and how much by the parents or how much students do on their own initiative, the students themselves best know. Some of the books they read outside of class are often no doubt of a rather high quality—and they are almost bound to be of a higher quality and more advanced than the selections in their readers. But some observations are perhaps due on this matter of outside reading. There is first of all the probability that the more difficult and the more important literary works are of more value to students in textbooks, where they can be studied by all with the help of a teacher. Second, the multitude of students who successfully avoid outside reading also successfully avoid reading much of literary value at all, because their readers don't have much. Third, for all the outside reading that some American students do, it is doubtful that on the whole it compares favorably in amount or in quality with what Soviet students read.

On this last point a statement in the recent U. S. government publication entitled *Soviet Commitment to Education* is telling. It reads as follows:

In a Kazan boarding school with grades 1-6 we [i.e., members of the "First Official U. S. Education Mission to the U.S.S.R."] asked the teacher of a 6th-grade literature class whether the children had reading difficulties. She said they did not and seemed to consider our question a little foolish because children had learned to read long before the 6th grade. She also told us that children in this school read, on the average, 100 books a year, that the curriculum required a minimum of 30 (books of 150-300 pp.) but that

73

some children read up to 150 books. They report on the books in class, in reading conferences, and sometimes at evening parties.

—*Soviet Commitment to Education.*
U. S. Department of Health, Education, and Welfare. Office of Education. Bulletin 1959, No. 16, p. 45.

It may be noted first of all that this sixth-grade teacher is not exaggerating when she says that Soviet students have learned to read long before the sixth grade. As we have seen, by the end of the fourth grade they have read enough and have acquired a large enough vocabulary to begin to study literature seriously in the fifth grade. Furthermore, since students will read on their own only when they have acquired the ability to read, the outside reading program, especially in the elementary grades, is tied directly to the methods used in teaching reading and to the quality of the readers themselves.

The truly amazing thing about the Kazan schoolteacher's description of the outside reading program in her schools is not that some students read 150 books a year or that on the average they read 100 books a year, for no doubt there are also American students who read as many books, but that all Soviet students are required to read 30 books a year. It is highly doubtful that this program of outside reading is matched in any sixth-grade class anywhere in the United States. Among the reasons that it is not matched is that our students are so handicapped by the meager 3,000- or 4,000-word reading vocabulary with which their readers have supplied them and by the way they are taught to read that they couldn't read 30 good-sized books a year if their lives depended upon it. The fact that a small percentage of elementary school students do read a great deal outside of class is obviously in spite of their readers, not because of them.

Something of the strength of the outside reading program in Soviet schools is further indicated in the official syllabi which deal specifically with the teaching of literature and which teachers are instructed to follow. In one of these syllabi the recognition of the importance of outside reading is stated as follows:

> Outside reading has an especially great significance: it teaches students to analyze books independently, it widens their horizons, develops their literary taste and enriches their knowledge of language. The teacher should make maximum use of this powerful means of education and enlightenment.
>
> —*Programmi srednei scholi, Russky yazik i literaturnie chtenie, v-vii klassi* (Programs of the middle schools, Russian language and literature, grades 5-7), p. 36.

The literature syllabi for grades five through ten contain lists of a large number of books recommended for outside reading. Each grade has a list, and each list is divided into four sections, as follows: (1) folklore, (2) Russian literature before 1917, (3) Soviet literature, and (4) foreign literature. The classical Russian authors are plentifully represented in these lists, as also, needless to say, are the Soviet authors; but of particular interest are the authors and books recommended from among foreign literatures. For the fifth grade, for example, the list includes Harriet Beecher Stowe's *Uncle Tom's Cabin,* Jules Verne's *Twenty Thousand Leagues under the Sea,* Daniel Defoe's *Robinson Crusoe,* Robert Louis Stevenson's *Treasure Island,* Mark Twain's *Tom Sawyer* and *Huckleberry Finn.* Among the foreign authors and titles listed for the sixth grade are James Fenimore Cooper's *The Pathfinder,* the stories of Jack London, Jonathan Swift's *Gulliver's Travels,* and Sir Walter Scott's *Ivanhoe;* those for the seventh grade include Dickens' *Oliver Twist,* Cervantes' *Don Quixote,* and selected works by Victor Hugo, James Fenimore Cooper, and Jack London. For the eighth grade, they include Shakespeare's *King Lear,* and Dickens'

*Pickwick Papers* and *Nicholas Nickleby;* for the ninth grade: Shakespeare's *Romeo and Juliet,* Dickens' *Dombey and Son,* and selected works by Beaumarchais, Schiller, Hugo, Balzac, and Maupassant; and for the tenth grade: Homer's *Iliad* and *Odyssey,* Aeschylus' *Prometheus Bound,* Shakespeare's Tragedies, and selected works from Goethe, Stendhal, Heine and Romain Rolland.

These are only some of the foreign authors and titles recommended to Soviet students for outside reading, and it is by no means safe to assume that only a few Soviet students read only a few of these books. The emphasis upon outside reading in Soviet schools is very great, and the full texts in translation of most of the above-mentioned titles and others are made easily available by the Soviet government for use in the schools.

Some comparisons between the outside reading program of American and Soviet schools seem in order. Inasmuch as American students are able to get from their fifth-grade readers only a 2,500-word vocabulary, and have a highly limited reading experience, they are ill equipped indeed to read *Treasure Island* or *Tom Sawyer,* much less *Huckleberry Finn* or *Robinson Crusoe*—unless they are among those who have learned to read despite the limitations of their readers. On the other hand, Soviet students are, as we have seen, well equipped to read these works in their entirety. The same fetters bind our students in the later grades and continue to bind them so long as their readers are merely readers and so long as the vocabulary in them is controlled.

The ironic but fortunate thing about the teaching of reading in our schools is that most students don't really learn to read from their readers, but rather from their history or geography or language books or from other books in which the vocabulary is not so carefully controlled and in which it is a good deal larger. Nonetheless, it is not only possible but even probable that more Soviet students at the end of the sixth grade have read more, and better, classics of English and American literature than our own students have at the same point in their education. The same may be equally true for the tenth grade. And there can be no question that Soviet students at the end of the tenth grade are better acquainted with foreign literatures than our students are at the end of the twelfth grade.

We perhaps need to remind ourselves from time to time how fortunate we are that English is our native language and that much of the world's best literature is written in our language. The extent of our good fortune may be brought home to us, for example, if we imagine ourselves living in a country with a little-known language and no significant literary heritage, or in a country where the literacy level is low or where good literature is difficult to obtain. Much of the population of the world exists in fact under some or all of these conditions. The United States suffers none of these deprivations. The English language is perhaps the greatest literary language in the world—not excepting Classical Greek; its literary achievements and its heritage are unsurpassed, the literacy level of the United States is among the highest in the world, and virtually everywhere in our country good literature is readily attainable either free or at modest cost. Yet, for all these blessings, there is no escaping the conclusion that the textbooks used in our grade schools and junior high schools present English as if it were an impoverished language, as if it had no literary heritage and no literary significance, and as if all our children were mentally defective.

# Fifth-Grade Soviet Literature Textbook

*Title:* RODNAYA LITERATURA (Native Literature)

NOTE: This fifth-grade literature text and the sixth- and seventh-grade texts that follow are used by *all* Soviet students whose native language is Russian

## CONTENTS

### PART I:   POPULAR ORAL WORKS

Two Fairy Tales (*6 pages*)
A discussion of the fairy tale as a literary type (*2 pages*)
Nineteen Riddles (*2 pages*)
A discussion of riddles (*1 page*)
Forty-two Proverbs (*4 pages*)

### PART II:   RUSSIAN WRITERS OF OUR COUNTRY'S PAST

### ALEXANDER PUSHKIN

Portrait of Pushkin
Biographical sketch of Pushkin (*8 pages*)
A short prose passage from Pushkin (*4 pages*)
A poem by Pushkin (*8 pages*)
A discussion of the tales of Pushkin, written by Maxim Gorky (*1 page*)
A poem by Pushkin (*1 page*)
A story by Pushkin called "The Snowstorm in the Steppes" (*3 pages*)

# Fifth-Grade American Reader

*Title:* A World to Enjoy
*Series:* THE MACMILLAN READERS (*supplementary reader*)
*Publisher:* The Macmillan Company
*Authors:* I. A. Gates and Celeste C. Peardon

## CONTENTS

### I LOVE A MYSTERY

An explanation of the epithet as a rhetorical device (*2 pages*)
A poem by Pushkin (*1 page*)
An explanation of "Narration, Description, and Dialogue"
  (*1 page*)
A poem by Pushkin (*1 page*)


# IVAN TURGENEV

Portrait of Turgenev
Biographical sketch of Turgenev (*9 pages*)
"Mumu," a story by Turgenev (*26 pages*)
A discussion of the tale as a literary form (*1 page*)
A discussion of the use of the simile (*1 page*)


# IVAN KRYLOV

Portrait of Krylov
Three fables by Krylov (*4 pages*)
A discussion of the metaphor and personification as literary
  devices (*1 page*)


# TARAS SHEVCHENKO

Portrait of Shevchenko
Biographical sketch of Shevchenko (*10 pages*)
Two short poems (*1 page*)


# IVAN GONCHAROV

Portrait of Goncharov
An excerpt from Goncharov's masterpiece *Oblomov* (*16 pages*)

## NICHOLAS NEKRASSOV

Portrait of Nekrassov
An excerpt from Nekrassov's epic *Jack Frost* (*10 pages*)


## MISCELLANEOUS

A description of spring by Leo Tolstoy (*1 page*)
A poem by Mikhail Lermontov (*2 pages*)
A discussion of the distinction between poetry and prose
    (*2 pages*)
A fable by Ivan Krylov (*2 pages*)
An explanation of the fable and the allegory as literary forms
    (*1 page*)
Proverbs and sayings from Krylov's fables (*1 page*)


## ANTON CHEKHOV

Portrait of Chekhov
"Kashtanka," a story by Chekhov (*18 pages*)


## MAXIM GORKY

Portrait of Gorky
"The Boys," a story by Gorky (*8 pages*)
"A Passion for Reading," a story by Gorky (*7 pages*)


## VLADIMIR KOROLENKO

Portrait of Korolenko
"Children of the Dungeon," a story by Korolenko (*28 pages*)

PART III: SOVIET WRITERS OF THE
SOVIET NATION

A tale by Alexander Fadeyev (*13 pages*)

A poem by S. Alymov (*1 page*)

An excerpt from the novel *The Young Guard* by Alexander
Fadeyev (*10 pages*)

A poem by M. Isakovsky (*2 pages*)

# Sixth-Grade Soviet Literature Textbook

*Title:* RODNAYA LITERATURA (Native Literature)

## CONTENTS

### PART I: FOLKLORE

An introduction explaining the origin and nature of folklore
A discussion of Russian popular epic poems
A short epic poem on the folk hero Ilya Murometz
A short discussion of popular folk heroes
A short epic poem "Volga and Mikyla"
A discussion of the poetical peculiarities of Russian popular
epic poems
A discussion of popular Russian songs
Four short songs
A discussion of the poetical characteristics of folk songs
A discussion of life as represented in Russian folklore
A statement of the significance of folklore

### PART II: LITERATURE OF THE NINETEENTH CENTURY

### IVAN KRYLOV

A portrait and a biographical sketch of Krylov (*3 pages*)
Four Fables of Krylov
A commentary on Krylov's *Fables* (*3 pages*)

### ALEXANDER PUSHKIN

A portrait and a biographical sketch of Pushkin (*10 pages*)

# Sixth-Grade American Reader

*Title:* *Bright Peaks*
*Series:* READING FOR MEANING
*Publisher:* Houghton Mifflin Company
*Authors:* Paul McKee, M. L. Harrison, Annie McCowen, and
Elizabeth Lehr

*From "Vocabulary" (printed in the back of the book)*

". . . repeats 78% of the vocabulary . . . of the previous books in
the series and introduces 876 new words . . . no group of 200 running words has more than six new words."

## CLASSIFIED CONTENTS

### BRAIN TEASERS

The Problem of the Tide
Can You Solve This?

### GAME

Strange Animals

### HOW-TO-MAKE-IT ARTICLE

Making Puzzles

### INFORMATION ARTICLES

Picnicking
Smoke Jumpers
How Birds Fly                          *Margaret Williamson*
Ski Contests
John Muir and the Loon                        *John Muir*
The Death Trap of the Ages            *Anne Terry White*

Five poems, each followed by a short discussion
*Dybrovsky*, a tale by Pushkin (*60 pages*)
A discussion of *Dybrovsky* (*6 pages*)


### MIKHAIL LERMONTOV

A portrait and a biographical sketch (*7 pages*)
A short poem followed by two pages of commentary
*Lay of the Czar Ivan the Terrible and the Merchant Kalashni-kov*, a poem by Lermontov, followed by 3 pages of commentary
A discussion of Russian versification (*3 pages*)


### NIKOLAI GOGOL

A portrait and a biographical sketch (*2 pages*)
*Taras Bulba*, a story by Gogol, here condensed to 55 pages and followed by a 6-page discussion of the story
An excerpt from "The Bewitched Spot," a story by Gogol (*2 pages*)
A brief discussion of kinds of literary works: the epic, the story, and the tale


### IVAN TURGENEV

A portrait and a biographical sketch (*2 pages*)
An excerpt from "Notes of a Hunter," a story by Turgenev (*17 pages*) followed by a 3-page discussion of the work
A discussion of the technique of narration in artistic works, i.e., straight narrative, description, and dialogue (*2 pages*)

# Seventh-Grade Soviet Literature Textbook

*Title:* RODNAYA LITERATURA (Native Literature)

## CONTENTS

### I. RUSSIAN WRITERS OF THE NINETEENTH CENTURY

### NICHOLAS NEKRASSOV

A portrait and a biographical sketch
"Reflections at the Main Entrance"
A discussion of the poem "Reflections at the Main Entrance"
"The Railroad"
A discussion of the poem "The Railroad"

### LEO TOLSTOY

A portrait and a biographical sketch
"Petya Rostov," a selection from Tolstoy's novel *War and Peace*

### ANTON CHEKHOV

A portrait and a biographical sketch
"Thick and Thin," a story by Chekhov
"The Chameleon," a story by Chekhov
Understanding Literary Types
Understanding Humor and Satire
The Significance of Russian Literature

# Seventh-Grade American Reader

*Title:* Doorways to Discovery
*Series:* THE GINN BASIC READERS
*Publishers:* Ginn and Company
*Authors:* David H. Russell, Mabel Snedaker, Doris Gates

## CONTENTS

### IT MIGHT HAPPEN TO YOU

### THE STORY BEHIND THE STORY

## II. SOVIET WRITERS

### MAXIM GORKY

A portrait and a biographical sketch
"Childhood," an excerpt from the story by Gorky
A discussion of the story "Childhood"
"A Song about Sokol," a story by Gorky
"A Song about Buryevyestnik," a story by Gorky

### VLADIMIR MAYAKOVSKY

A portrait and a biographical sketch
"An Unusual Adventure," a poem by Mayakovsky
A discussion of the poem "An Unusual Adventure"
An excerpt from Mayakovsky's poem "Fire"
The Peculiarities of Mayakovsky's Poetic Skill

### NICHOLAS OSTROVSKY

A portrait and a biographical sketch
An excerpt from Ostrovsky's novel *The Tempering of the Steel*
A discussion of the novel *The Tempering of the Steel*

### DZHAMBIL DZHABAEV

A Lullaby

93

# Eighth-Grade Soviet Literature Anthology

*Title:* RUSSKAYA LITERATURA (Russian Literature)

*This textbook is an anthology of Russian literature from its beginnings to about 1850.*

## CONTENTS

### PART I: THE LITERATURE OF ANCIENT RUSSIA

Six excerpts from Old Russian Chronicles; An Heroic Epic (*Old Russian and Modern Russian in a side-by-side translation*); Two short prose accounts of medieval historical events

### PART II: LITERATURE OF THE EIGHTEENTH CENTURY

### MIKHAIL LOMONOSOV

One poem

### GABRIEL DERZHAVIN

Three poems

### DENIS IVANOVICH FONVIZIN

*The Young Hopeful,* a play in five acts (*condensed*)

# Eighth-Grade American Reader

*Title: Adventures for Readers: Book 2*
*Series:* ADVENTURES IN LITERATURE PROGRAM (Olympic Edition)
*Publisher:* Harcourt, Brace and Company, Inc.

## CONTENTS

*(Table of Contents is reprinted here in shortened form in order
to stress the authors of the selections)*

## ALEXANDER RADISHCHEV

*Voyage from Petersburg to Moscow,* a novel (*excerpt*); a letter (*excerpt*); "Freedom," a poem (*condensed*)

## NIKOLAI KARAMZIN

"Poor Liza," a story (*condensed*)

### PART III: LITERATURE OF THE NINETEENTH CENTURY

## VASSILY ZHUKOVSKY

Three poems

## KONDRATEY RILYEYEV

Four poems

## ALEXANDER BRIBOYEDOV

*The Folly of Being Wise,* a play (*excerpt*); an essay by Ivan Goncharov on the play *The Folly of Being Wise*

## ALEXANDER PUSHKIN

Nineteen poems; one short play; *Eugene Onegin,* a verse novel (*condensed to 80 pages*); *Boris Godunov,* a play in verse

Catton; Stephen Foster; Rosemary and Stephen Vincent Benét; An Old Sea Chantey; Mark Twain (*10 pages* of *Cub Pilot on the Mississippi*)

### V. AMERICA NOT SO LONG AGO

Robert Frost; J. Frank Dobie; Two Western Songs; Carl Sandburg; Clarence Day; John Steinbeck (*A Model T Named "IT"*); George and Helen Papashvily; Charles A. Lindbergh

### VI. MAKERS OF MODERN AMERICA

William Bridgeman and Jacqueline Hazard; Mildred Plew Meigs; C. B. Wall; Ira Wolfert; Eric Berger; H. J. Rand

### VII. FAVORITE AMERICAN STORIES

O. Henry; Mark Twain (*Tom Sawyer: The Glorious Whitewasher*, adapted for television by Alvin Sapinsley); Telling a Favorite Story in a New Way (*a picture story*); Edward Everett Hale; Washington Irving (*The Legend of Sleepy Hollow*)

### VIII. FAVORITE AMERICAN POEMS

John Greenleaf Whittier; Oliver Wendell Holmes; Walt Whitman; Emily Dickinson; Robert Frost; Henry Wadsworth Longfellow (*Evangeline*)

### IX. SUSPENSE AND DANGER

Hunt Miller; "Tenzing of Everest" and James Ramsey Ullman; Alfred, Lord Tennyson; Robert Browning; Sir Walter Scott; David Grinwell; Mary Roberts Rinehart

### X. THE WORLD OF NATURE

Anya Seton; William Shakespeare (*Under the Greenwood Tree*); Jesse Stuart; Emily Dickinson; Robert Frost; Ruth

(*condensed to 48 pages*); *The Captain's Daughter,* a novel
(*80 pages*)

## VISSARION BELINSKY

An essay on the works of Alexander Pushkin (*excerpt*)

## MIKHAIL LERMONTOV

Twelve poems; *A Hero of Our Time,* a novel (*condensed to
100 pages*)

## VISSARION BELINSKY

An essay "On *A Hero of Our Time*" (*excerpt*)

## NIKOLAI GOGOL

*The Inspector General,* a play; *Dead Souls,* a novel (*condensed
to 100 pages*)

## VISSARION BELINSKY

Six essays; two letters

Elizabeth Tanner; Richard Armour; Percy Bysshe Shelley; Carl Sandburg; Melvine Cane; O. A. Battista; Robert P. Tristram Coffin; Edwin Way Teale; William Wordsworth

### XI. THE YEARS AHEAD

Oscar Schisgall; William O. Douglas; E-Yeh-Shure; Pearl S. Buck; Edward Hodnett; Jessamyn West; Dwight D. Eisenhower

# Ninth-Grade Soviet Literary History Textbook

*This text is an account of Russian literature from about 1860 to 1900, arranged chiefly according to author. The Table of Contents is here slightly condensed.*

# Ninth-Grade American Reader

*Title: Adventures in Reading*
*Series:* THE ADVENTURES IN LITERATURE PROGRAM (Olympic edition)
*Publisher:* Harcourt, Brace and Company, Inc.

## CONTENTS

*(Table of Contents is reprinted here in shortened form in order to
indicate chiefly the authors of the selections)*

### VII. POETS OF "THE PURE ART"

Afanasi Shenshin-Fet. Apollon Maikov.

### VIII. FEDOR TIUTCHEV

### IX. BIOGRAPHY AND MUSIC
### OF THE SIXTIES

### X. IVAN GONCHAROV

His Life and Works. His Childhood and Youth. His University Years. In Service. The Beginning of His Literary Activities. "A Common Story." New Literary Plans. His Voyage around the World. The Completion of his Novel *Oblomov*. New Service Activity and Resignation. "The Precipice." The Last Years of His Life. Goncharov's Trilogy. The Novel *Oblomov* (*an 18-page discussion*).

### XI. ALEXANDER OSTROVSKY

His Life and Works. His Childhood and Youth. In Service. The Beginning of His Dramatic Activity. "Bankrupt." The Works of Ostrovsky in the Fifties. Noblemen and Industrialists of a New Type in the Plays of Ostrovsky. "The Ice-maiden." The Life of Ostrovsky from 1860 to 1880. The play *The Thunderstorm* (*a 15-page discussion*). The Significance of Ostrovsky.

### XII. IVAN TURGENEV

A Biographical Sketch. "Notes of a Hunter." The Novels of Turgenev: *Rudin. A Nest of Gentlefolk. On the Eve.* The Novel *Fathers and Sons* (*a 12-page discussion*). His Stories and Tales. Turgenev's Last Works. The Significance of the Works of Turgenev.

Mary Austin; Jessamyn West; Willa Cather; Rosemary and Stephen Vincent Benét; Witter Bynner; Emily Dickinson; Edna St. Vincent Millay; Lew Sarett; Stephen Vincent Benét; Amy Lowell; Carl Sandburg; Robert Frost

### III. ADVENTURES IN REALITY

Wolfgang Langewiesche; Katherine B. Shippen; Amelia Earhart; Hermann Hagedorn; Charles Coombs; Lynn Poole; Lloyd C. Douglas; Mary Ellen Chase; Jesse Stuart; Salom Rizk; Carl Sandburg; Rackham Holt; Rice E. Cochran; Corey Ford; Stephen B. Leacock; Royal Dixon; Charles Laughton

### IV. THE CURTAIN RISES

*The Stolen Prince*, a one-act play by Dan Totheroh; *Never Come Monday*, a radio play by Eric Knight and Stephen Fox; *The Valiant*, a one-act play by Holworthy Hall and Robert Middlemass; *The Dancers*, a television play by Horton Foote

### V. THE EPIC TALE

*The Odyssey*, seven selections in verse

### VI. THE NOVEL

*Great Expectations* by Charles Dickens "as abridged by Blanche Jennings Thompson"

### XIII. NICHOLAS CHERNYSHEVSKY

His Life. His Childhood and Youth. After His University Years. Chernyshevsky as Editor of "The Contemporary." Chernyshevsky in Prison. In Exile. The Last Years of Chernyshevsky's Life. His Novel *What Is to Be Done?* Prototypes of the Heroes of *What Is to Be Done?* Chernyshevsky's Aesthetic Theories. The Peculiarities of his Language. The Polemical Character of the Novel. *What Is to Be Done?* and the Literary-Political Struggle of the Sixties and Seventies.

### XIV. NICHOLAS NEKRASSOV

His Childhood and Youth. The Petersburg Ordeal. His Friendship with Belinsky. Nekrassov as Editor of "The Contemporary." Nekrassov during the Sixties. Music in the Poetry of Nekrassov. "Poet and Citizen." "Elegy." The City Motif in the Works of Nekrassov. His Poem *Who Finds Life Good in Russia?* The Representation of Women Peasants in His Poetry. The Artistic Peculiarities of the Poem *Who Finds Life Good in Russia?* The Significance of the Works of Nekrassov

### XV. THE DECADES OF THE SEVENTIES AND EIGHTIES

The Political Struggle in the Seventies. Artistic Literature of the Seventies. Feodor Dostoyevsky. Nicholas Leskov. The General Character of Literature in the Eighties. Semion Nadson. Vselovod Garshin. Biography and Sculpture. Music

### XVI. MIKHAIL SALTYKOV-SHCHEDRIN

His Life. His Childhood and Youth. The Beginning of His Literary Activity. Shchedrin as Editor of "The Contemporary." The Last Years of His Life. His "History of a Town." His Novel

*The Golovlyovs.* His "Fairy Tales." The Significance of the Works of Shchedrin.

### XVII.   LEO TOLSTOY

A Biographical Sketch. His Childhood. His Youth. After His University Years. Military Service and the Beginning of His Literary Activity. "Childhood." "Boyhood." "Youth." "Tales of Sebastopol." "The Cossacks." Tolstoy as Teacher. The Creation of the Novel *War and Peace. Anna Karenina.* In Yasnaya Polyana. The Last Years of His Life. The Novel *Resurrection.* The Death of Tolstoy. The Novel *War and Peace* (*a 20-page discussion*). An Appraisal of Tolstoy by Vladimir Ilych Lenin. Tolstoy and World Literature.

### XVIII.   ANTON CHEKOV

A Biographical Sketch. His Childhood and High School Years. His University Years and the Beginning of His Literary Activity. His Illness. His Life in Yalta. The Death of Chekhov. Chekhov's Stories (*a 10-page discussion*). Chekhov as a Master of the Realistic Story. Chekhov as a Dramatist. The Play *The Cherry Orchard* (*a 15-page discussion*).

### XIX.   THE WORLD-WIDE SIGNIFICANCE OF RUSSIAN CLASSICAL LITERATURE

# Tenth-Grade Soviet Literature Anthology

## CONTENTS

### I.  INTRODUCTION

Vladimir Ilych Lenin on Party Literature; Vladimir Ilych Lenin on Culture and Art. The Second All-Union Conference of Soviet Writers

### II.  MAXIM GORKY

"The Old Woman," a story (*13 pages, condensed*); *The Lower Depths*, a play (*60 pages, slightly condensed*); *Mother*, a novel (*80 pages, selected chapters*). "Vladimir Ilych Lenin" (*20 pages, condensed*)

### III.  VLADIMIR MAYAKOVSKY

Ten poems (*50 pages*)

### IV.  NICHOLAS OSTROVSKY

*The Tempering of the Steel*, a novel (*50 pages, excerpts*)

### V.  MIKHAIL SHOLOKHOV

*The Virgin Soil Upturned*, a novel (*80 pages, selected chapters*)

### VI.  ALEXANDER FADEYEV

*The Young Guard*, a novel (*115 pages, selected chapters*); "My Work on the Novel *The Young Guard*"; On Soviet Literature

### VII.  ALEXANDER TVARDOVSKY

*Vassily Tyorkin*, a poem (*15 pages, excerpts*)

# Tenth-Grade American Literature Anthology

*Title: Adventures in Appreciation*
*Series:* ADVENTURES IN LITERATURE PROGRAM (Mercury Edition)
*Publisher:* Harcourt, Brace and Company, Inc.

## CONTENTS

*(Table of Contents is reprinted here in shortened form in order
to indicate chiefly the authors of the selections)*

### I. SHORT STORIES

Walter D. Edmonds; Marc Connelly; O. Henry; Kurt Vonnegut, Jr.; Stephen Vincent Benét; T. O. Beachcroft; Mary E. Wilkins Freeman; Albert Richard Wetjen; William Saroyan; Marjorie Kinnan Rawlings; Michael Fessier; Jessamyn West; Wilbur Schramm; Saki (H. H. Munro); Howard Brubaker; Selma Lagerlöf; Anton Chekhov; Jean C. Becket; John Galsworthy

### II. POETRY

John Masefield; Edna St. Vincent Millay; A. E. Housman; Alfred Noyes; Henry Wadsworth Longfellow; Lord Byron; John Masefield; Edgar Allen Poe; old Scottish ballad; Roy Helton; Rudyard Kipling; Elizabeth Coatsworth; Lord Byron; W. H. Auden; Johann Wolfgang von Goethe; Vachel Lindsay; William Butler Yeats; Francis Orray Ticknor; Arthur Guiterman; Edward Rolland Sill; Stephen Vincent Benét; Edna St. Vincent Millay; Walt Whitman; Anna Wickham; Carl Sandburg; Edwin Markham; Negro spiritual; Robert P. Tristram Coffin; Sara Teasdale; Einar Skjaeraasen; John Gould Fletcher; Emily Dickinson; Carl Sandburg; Helen Wadell; Ogden Nash; Lewis Carroll; W. S. Gilbert; Phyllis McGinley; James Whitcomb Riley; Robert Burns; Jan Struther; Robert Frost; John Donne

VIII.   MIKHAIL ISAKOVSKY

Two poems

IX.   O. GONCHAR

"The Standard-Bearers," a story (*20 pages*)

### III. NONFICTION

Mark Twain (*I Ride a Bucking Horse*); Gretchen Finletter; James Thurber; A. C. M. Azoy; Herman Melville (*The Bonhomme Richard*); Robert J. Casey; Edna Yost; Antoine de Saint-Exupéry; Winston Churchill; Thor Heyerdahl; James Ramsey Ullman; Jim Corbett; Vilhjalmur Stefansson; Pierre J. Huss; Stephen Leacock; Robert Benchley; E. B. White

### IV. THE DRAMA

*Sunday Costs Five Pesos,* a short play by Josephina Niggli; *The Will,* a short play by James M. Barrie; *Julius Caesar* (*complete*) by William Shakespeare

### V. THE LITERARY EPIC

Introductions: The Literary Epic, Alfred, Lord Tennyson; *Idylls of the King* (*four selections*)

### VI. THE NOVEL

Introductions: The Novel, George Eliott; *Silas Marner* (*complete*) by George Eliot

# 3

## FOREIGN LANGUAGES
## IN SOVIET AND AMERICAN
## SCHOOLS

In the matter of foreign-language training, there can be no doubt that American schools have a sorry record indeed compared either to Soviet schools or to the schools in any other European country. The weakness of foreign-language training in our schools is to a degree understandable, because the United States suffers from severe linguistic isolation. Much of the population can go for years at a time, perhaps even a whole lifetime, without hearing anyone speak a foreign language or seeing any publication written in a foreign language. Furthermore, Americans have always capitalized upon the willingness of people in other countries to learn English, and the attitude is common that non-English-speaking people have an obligation to learn our language but that we have no obligation to learn theirs. Such conditions, however, and such attitudes will no longer excuse the appalling linguistic ignorance of the citizens of a country which has become the leader of the free world, especially in these times.

One way of understanding the state of foreign languages in our schools at the present time is to make some comparisons between the percentage of students who are now taking foreign languages with the percentage who were studying them fifty years ago. Latin, of course, has suffered the greatest decline. In 1910 as many as 49 per cent of high school students were studying Latin, whereas now less than 8 per cent are studying it. But the modern languages have suffered almost as severely: whereas approximately 24 per cent of high school students were taking German in 1910, less than 2 per cent are taking it now; over 15 per cent of high school students were taking French as late as 1922, but only 6 per cent are studying it now. Even Spanish has declined from 11 per cent in 1922 to about 9 per cent at the present time. The percentage of students studying Italian or Russian or any other language than those mentioned is infinitesimal. Forty-nine per cent of the public high schools in the United States do not even offer a modern foreign language.*

In terms of total figures, the unhappy facts are that in 1910 84 per cent, or about five out of six students, were studying a foreign language, whereas about 25 per cent, or one out of four students, are studying one now.

But these statistics do not tell the whole story. Much more disheartening is the fact that of the meager 25 per cent who do study a foreign language in high school, approximately 90 per cent do so for only two years. And since even the most optimistic foreign-language teachers have to admit that two years of a foreign language at the high school level are by no means sufficient to enable a student to speak, read, or write it with any degree of proficiency, no more than 3 per cent of all students who attend high school (namely, those who study a language for three or four years) are able to acquire any degree of skill in it. This number would be slightly increased if one included college students who continue with the same language they studied in high school, but even at the college level nine

* See John F. Latimer, *What's Happened to Our High Schools* (Public Affairs Press, Washington, D. C., 1958), pp. 26-27. See also *Modern Foreign Languages in the High School* (U. S. Department of Health, Education, and Welfare. Office of Education. Bulletin 1958, No. 16), pp. 42-44.

out of ten students study a foreign language for only two years.

These statistics present a deplorable picture, and they bring great shame upon our schools, particularly at a time when foreign language training ought to be at an all-time high rather than at an all-time low.

An examination of the foreign-language curriculum in Soviet schools will serve to point up the extent of the weaknesses in foreign-language teaching in the United States, even without considering the content of the respective foreign-language courses.

The unhappiest comparison comes from the fact that whereas only 25 per cent of American high school students study a foreign language and 90 per cent of those do so for only two years, *all* Soviet students study a foreign language, and in the regular ten-year schools they study it continuously for six years. They begin the study of a foreign language in the fifth grade and they continue with the same language until they have finished the tenth grade. They are permitted to choose English or German or French. Some 45 per cent choose English, 35 per cent choose German, and about 20 per cent choose French. In the new eleven-year schools they will study one of these languages for seven consecutive years.

Fifth-grade students begin at once with a foreign-language textbook which combines a study of grammar with practice in reading in the language. Considerable attention is also given to both pronunciation and conversation in the classroom, especially in these early grades, but the students' work in a foreign language, even in the fifth grade, is concerned chiefly with the material in their textbook.

In their first year of German or French, for example, they learn the alphabet and some of the rudiments of the grammar of these languages and they are given practice in both reading and writing about 400 words. Here, for example, is a reading lesson in German in the *fifth*-grade textbook used in Soviet schools.

### Die Söhne

Am Brunnen stehen drei Frauen. Ihre Eimer sind voll Wasser. Da sitzt auch ein Mann. Die Frauen stehen am Brunnen und sprechen über ihre Söhne.

Die erste Frau sagt: "Mein Sohn singt schön. Kein Knabe im Dorf singt so schön wie er."

Die zweite Frau sagt: "Mein Sohn ist stark. Kein Knabe im Dorf ist so stark wie er."

Die dritte Frau aber schweigt. Die anderen Frauen fragen sie: "Warum schweigst du?"

Da antwortet die dritte Frau: "Mein Sohn ist nicht stark. Er singt auch nicht schön."

Der Mann hört das Gespräch der Frauen. Die Frauen nehmen ihre Eimer und gehen nach Hause. Da sehen sie auf der Strasse drei Knaben. Das sind ihre Söhne. Der erste Knabe singt ein Lied. Der zweite macht einen Handstand. Der dritte Knabe aber nimmt die Eimer der Mutter und trägt sie nach Hause. Die Frauen sagen zu dem Mann: "Siehst du, Grossvater, das sind unsere Söhne!" Der Mann aber antwortet: "Söhne? Ich sehe hier nur einen Sohn."

And here is a similar fifth-grade reading lesson in French:

### Deux Amis

Maman est dans sa chambre. Elle lit un livre. Elle entend un grand bruit. Elle écoute: une chaise tombe, les garçons crient, Nina pleure. Maman va dans la chambre des enfants. Elle ouvre la porte. Maman demande:

—Pourquoi pleures-tu, Nina?

—Mon chat! Mimi! Où est Mimi?

Nicholas est près de la fenêtre. Il dit:

—Ton chat est dans la cour. Regarde, il est sur cet arbre.

Maman s'approche de la fenêtre. Elle voit Mimi sur un arbre. Elle appelle:

—Mimi! Mimi!

Mimi saute sur la fenêtre. Maman prend Mimi dans ses bras. Elle dit à Nicolas:

—Prends ton chien dans les bras.

Nicolas prend Ami dans ses bras et s'approche de Maman. Elle caresse le chat. Elle caresse le chien. Elle dit à Nina:

—Apporte une assiette avec du lait.

Nina apporte une assiette avec du lait. Elle pose l'assiette à terre. Maman pose Mimi à terre. Voilà le nez du chat dans l'assiette. Nicolas pose son chien à terre. Ami met le nez dans l'assiette. Maman caresse le chien et la chat. Ils mangent dans la même assiette.

Training in the grammar and the reading and writing of German or French continues through the tenth grade, along with some practice in conversation, until the students have something like a mastery of the grammar of either of these languages (which after all is relatively simple compared to the complexities of Russian grammar) and a reading vocabulary of about 2,500 words.

In direct contrast to the procedure in many American elementary schools, Soviet students are taught to read English by the phonics method. They are told at the outset that the English language has 26 letters which represent 44 basic sounds, and by the time they have finished the text used in the fifth grade, they are not only expected to have mastered the letters and sounds, but they have considerable training in reading, writing, translating, and speaking about 400 words. This means that Soviet students at the end of their first year of the study of English can learn more about written English than our own students can learn from their first-grade readers, which, it will be recalled, usually have a vocabulary of only a little more than 300 words. In fact, in the matter of reading vocabulary, many American readers do not pull ahead of Soviet English-language textbooks until the fourth or fifth year. Furthermore, Soviet students may find their elementary reading lessons in English more interesting than our students find theirs. Here, for example, is a passage from an adaptation of Mark Twain's *The Prince and the Pauper,* which appears in the Soviet second-year English text:

> The prince thought a little about Tom Canty's words. Then he said: "Is your life very hard at Offal Court?"
>
> "No, not very hard. Only when I am hungry. We have very little food sometimes. But we boys in Offal Court often laugh and play. In the summer we have very much time to play. We often play in the river."
>
> "Oh, I want to do that too!" cried the prince. "Tell me more."
>
> "We dance and we sing near the river, we play in the water and . . ."
>
> "I want very much to play in the water!" cried the prince. "I want to have your clothes. I want to walk without shoes. I want to play in the water."
>
> "And I want very much to put on your beautiful clothes," cried Tom.
>
> "Listen, boy; you put on my clothes for a few minutes and I shall put on your clothes," said the prince, "but only for a few minutes."

It may be that there are American sixth graders who would have difficulty getting through this passage.

It is important to note, too, that the reading selections in these foreign-language texts become increasingly literary in the higher grades, and numerous selections deal with the historical and cultural aspects of the countries in which the languages are spoken natively. The ninth- and tenth-grade German textbooks, for example, have selections about Schiller, Goethe, and Heinrich Heine, and stories or poems by them, though often in adapted form. Needless to say, information about Marx and Engels is not omitted. Similarly, the French textbooks of the upper grades have numerous selections by and about Victor Hugo, Balzac, Émile Zola, Anatole France, Maupassant, and Flaubert.

Of particular interest are literary selections which appear in the Soviet students' English textbooks in the upper grades, because they serve to emphasize once again the lack of literary value of American readers in the elementary and junior high grades.

The second-year English text used in the sixth grade in Soviet schools, for example, has selections with far greater literary value than those which appear in the sixth-grade readers in American schools. There are, in addition to the adaptation of Mark Twain's *Prince and the Pauper,* an adaptation of Oscar Wilde's "The Selfish Giant," and some animal fables which must seem incomparably more exciting to Soviet students than anything our elementary school students are likely to find in their readers.

The third-year English readers (seventh grade) used in Soviet schools introduce students to some of the masterpieces of English and American literature, including a summary of the story of *Robinson Crusoe, Jane Eyre,* and *The Pickwick Papers,* as well as of *Tom Sawyer* and *Uncle Tom's Cabin.* Selections in the fourth-, fifth-, and sixth-year English-language textbooks include summaries of Dickens' *Our Mutual Friend,* Jonson's *Volpone,* Shakespeare's *King Lear,* and excerpts from Thackeray's *The Rose and the Ring,* George Eliot's *The Mill on the Floss,* Pepys' *Diary* (on the great fire of London), Oscar Wilde's *The Devoted Friend,* Hardy's *Tess of the D'Urbervilles,* and selections from Jerome K. Jerome, H. G. Wells, John Galsworthy, and George Bernard Shaw. There are lyric poems by Shakespeare, Burns, Wordsworth, Thomas Moore, and Byron, and there are short accounts of some of the most important English writers, and portraits of Shakespeare, Defoe, Fielding, Scott, Shelley, Byron, Dickens, and Thackeray.

All this means simply that Soviet students who study English in these grades are certain to be learning more about English literature from their English-language texts than our elementary school students are learning from theirs.

Such, then, is the foreign-language program in the Soviet schools. How favorably does the foreign-language program in our own schools compare with it?

One dramatic way of answering this question is to imagine how many American students in the fifth or sixth grades could read the French or German passages reprinted on pages 115-116 or a similar passage in Spanish or any other foreign language. The few public schools that have begun to experiment with the study of foreign languages in the upper grades of elementary school do not concentrate on teaching the students to read the language.

It would be quite difficult to find an eighth-grade student who could read these passages as a result of attending our schools, because, except in rare instances, American eighth-grade students are still not being taught to read a foreign language. And as we have seen, three-fourths of our high school graduates cannot read such passages either, because they have never studied a foreign language at all.

It is perhaps even more embarrassing to conjecture how many parents or teachers or even school administrators can read these passages or similar passages in another foreign language. The number, one suspects, is distressingly small. Or, when students or parents or teachers or school administrators are found who can read these passages, can they also read this somewhat more difficult passage which appears in the Soviet eighth-grade German text?

### Der Geheimnisvolle Verfolger

Der Schneider Schlorke, der in einem kleinen Städtchen lebte, kehrte von einer Reise zurück. Er ging vom Bahnhof nach Hause.

119

Es war gegen Mitternacht, und der Weg war schlecht beleuchtet. Plötzlich bemerkte der Schneider einen Mann, der ihm folgte. Schlorke ging schneller, aber der Mann hinter ihm tat es auch. Da ging er langsamer, aber sein Verfolger ging auch langsamer. Nun kamen sie in die Nähe eines Gartens. Herr Schlorke versuchte eine Kriegslist: er lief schnell in den Garten und hoffte, sich auf diese Weise von seinem Verfolger zu befreien. Der Mann kam jedoch auch in den Garten. Halbtot vor Angst lief Herr Schlorke schnell durch die Alleen des Gartens, aber der Mann blieb ihm dicht auf den Fersen. Endlich drehte sich Herr Schlorke um und fragte voll Angst: "Erlauben Sie mal . . . Was wollen Sie von mir?" "Ach, verzeihen Sie," antwortete der Fremde, "ich wollte Frau Mühlbach ein Paket bringen und fragte am Bahnhof nach dem Wege. Da sagte der Bahnbeamte zu mir: 'Gehen Sie nur immer diesem Herrn nach; er wohnt in demselben Haus!' "

Or this from the corresponding Soviet eighth-grade French text:

### Matéo Falcone

Cependant Matéo et sa femme parurent sur le sentier. En voyant les soldats Matéo s'avança vers la maison. L'adjudant vint au devant de lui.—Bon jour, frère, dit-il. Nous avons de la chance aujourd'hui. Et il raconta qu'ils avaient arrêté Gianetto. "Il s'était bien caché, dit-il, mais le petit Fortunato nous a aidé à le trouver."

Gianetto sourit d'un sourire étrange en voyant Matéo Falcone; puis se tournant vers la porte de la maison, il cracha sur le seuil, en disant: "Maison d'un traître!"

Matéo, accablé, porta sa main au front.

Les soldats emportèrent le bandit blessé.

Fortunato jeta un coup d'oeil inquiet sur le père qui le regardait avec colère.

—Tu commences bien! dit-il enfin d'une voix calme, mais effrayante.

—Mon père! s'écria l'enfant en s'avançant, les larmes aux yeus. Mais Matéo cria:

—Arrière de moi!

L'enfant s'arrêta, immobile à quelques pas de son père et éclata en sanglots.

Giuseppa, la mère de Fortunato, s'approcha. Elle vit la chaîne de la montre qui sortait de la chemise de Fortunato et lui demanda d'un ton sévère, qui lui avait donné cette montre.

Le garçon répondit que c'était l'adjudant.

Falcone saisit la montre, le jeta avec force contre une pierre et la mit en mille morceaux.

Il rejeta son fusil sur l'épaule et se dirigea dans la forêt en criant à Fortunato de la suivre. L'enfant obéit. Giuseppa courut après Matéo et lui saisit le bras.

—C'est ton fils, lui dit-elle d'une voix tremblante.

—Laisse-moi, je suis son père, répondit Matéo.

Giuseppa embrassa son fils et rentra en pleurant dans la maison.

Falcone marcha dans le sentier; il s'arrêta dans un petit ravin.

—Fortunato, va auprès de la grosse pierre, ordonna-t-il.

L'enfant obéit, il se mit à genoux.

—Oh, mon père! Grâce! Pardonnez-moi! Je ne le ferai plus . . .

Il parlait encore, il essaya de se relever et d'embrasser les genoux de son père.

Mais il n'eut pas le temps . . . Matéo fit feu, et Fortunato tomba raide mort.

*—Adapted from Prosper Mérimée*

One does not have to be a college professor to be able to read foreign-language passages comparable to these reprinted here. Soviet students who get through the eighth grade can read them and so can almost any other European student who gets through the eighth grade. Needless to say, the selections from the ninth- and tenth-grade foreign-language texts in the Russian schools are considerably more advanced than these.

It may be noted too that the foreign-language requirements in Soviet schools are modest compared to those in the schools of other European countries. Soviet students are required to study only one foreign language if their native language is Russian; if it is not, they must study Russian and another foreign language as well. But the typical European *gymnasium* requires as many as two, three, or four foreign languages, depending upon the country and the curriculum in which the student is enrolled. Thus, among the highly civilized countries of the world, the linguistic ignorance of the United States is in a profound and distressing sense unique.

While eighth-grade Soviet students have advanced as far with a foreign language as the above-quoted passages suggest, virtually none of our students, except some in private schools and an insignificant number of public and parochial schools, have even begun to read a foreign language in school. But as we have seen, about a fourth of them do take a foreign language somewhere between the ninth and the twelfth grades. Here, over a two-year period, they learn the rudiments of the grammar of a foreign language and they acquire a reading vocabulary which, though not large enough to enable them to read a language comfortably, at least gives them a good start. There is often vigorous emphasis upon conversation, sometimes, however, at the expense of the written language. A very small percentage go on to study a third and perhaps a fourth year of a language, the minimum amount of time necessary to acquire a satisfying knowledge of it.

Some high school foreign-language teachers do very well indeed with the little time they have to try to teach students a foreign language. Nonetheless, regardless of how excellent the teacher or the textbooks may be, two years of a foreign language at the high school level is wholly inadequate, and it can be said that virtually no high school student after his two-year course can read or write, much less speak, a foreign language with any degree of competence. Even two years of a foreign language at the college level rarely provides any real competence either in reading or in speaking the language.

Foreign-language teachers have long recognized the inadequacy of the foreign-language program in our schools, but they have been working against tremendous opposition in their attempts to improve it. The recommendation has often been made—and is being made more frequently and more loudly now—that high school students should study a foreign language for four years rather than two. The Modern Language Association even advocates that students begin to study a language as early as the fourth grade and continue with the same language through the twelfth. These proposals stem partly from the realization that foreign languages are of immense importance because of the major contribution they make to our children's liberal education and to their skill in using language. They also stem from the realization that the tremendous advances in communication and transportation, and the rise of the United States as leader of the free world and the main bulwark against the threat of communism have made it mandatory that large numbers of Americans acquire a *good* knowledge of at least one foreign language.

It is only fair to say that a few schools in the country have made some effort to respond to the great need for thorough foreign-language training in the curriculum. Experiments have been particularly lively on the elementary level, where more and more schools are taking steps, though timid and uncertain, to introduce foreign-language instruction as early as the fourth or fifth grade. I would point out, however, to those who are proud of the gains that our schools have made in the past two years in foreign-language instruction, that these gains are still pitifully meager.

It is important to note, however, that in the vast majority of these elementary school experiments in foreign-language teaching the procedure is almost diametrically opposed to the way foreign languages are taught in Soviet schools and in European schools generally. The basic difference between the European method and the American method is that European students (including, as we have seen, Soviet students) use textbooks from the very beginning, and from them they learn the grammar of the language. They are given considerable practice both in reading and writing the language even in the early grades. They have textbooks for each grade, beginning often with the fifth grade; and in each grade the grammar, the reading selections, and the writing exercises become increasingly difficult. Attention is, of course, given to pronunciation and there are signs that greater emphasis is being given to conversation, but European students learn a foreign language chiefly through the use of textbooks.

The overwhelming tendency in American elementary schools, on the other hand, is to teach foreign languages without any textbooks at all, and in fact the most widely approved methods forbid the written word in any form whatsoever in the classroom in the early grades: the entire effort is directed toward trying to teach children to speak a foreign language, the idea being that speaking should come before reading. Whether or not it is actually possible to teach students to speak a foreign language merely through classroom experience or even, at the high school level, with the aid of a "language laboratory," remains to be seen.

In any case, it is evident that the primary problem of foreign-language teaching in our schools is one of curriculum rather than methods. There are not nearly enough students studying a foreign language, and those who are do not study it nearly long enough, nor do they start early enough. Undoubtedly one of the most effective ways of improving foreign-language instruction in the schools is for the colleges and universities to raise their foreign-language entrance requirements. Perhaps nothing accounts so readily for the sorry state of language instruction in our schools as the fact that, as the Modern Language Association reported in a 1958 survey of 1,005 accredited four-year colleges and universities, only 28.3 per cent of those offering a B.A. degree have a foreign language entrance requirement and only 23.1 per cent of those offering a B.S. degree had such a requirement.* The MLA report issued in September 1960 shows an insignificant gain on this score and observes that even now "more than two-thirds of American colleges will accept students for admission who have never been exposed to a language other than their mother tongue."

These facts severely limit the incentive for our high schools to increase the foreign-language requirement. Furthermore, it is likely that so long as a foreign language remains an elective in our high schools, students will continue to avoid studying it. But one thing in all this is abundantly clear: until major curricular changes are made in our schools in favor of much more time devoted to foreign-language study, the traditional linguistic ignorance of this country will remain traditional—and an increasingly heavy liability.

* See *Publications of the Modern Language Association*, Vol. LXXIV, No. 4, part 2 (September, 1959), p. 34.

# 4

## HISTORY
## IN SOVIET AND AMERICAN
## SCHOOLS

Since no man can understand the century or the age in which he lives unless he can compare it with other centuries and other ages, history is one of the most important of all areas of human knowledge. How much our own times are like former times and how much they differ from former times are questions which only a systematic and thorough study of history can answer. The best evidence that a nation has to show that its people "never had it so good" is the evidence of history, the best evidence of the consummate evil of tyranny is the evidence of history, the best evidence of the preciousness of freedom is the evidence of history, the best evidence of the superiority of the democratic way of life is the evidence of history, and the best evidence of a thousand other truths about men and institutions is the evidence of history. Therefore, the nation that underestimates the importance of history invites disaster, especially in these times.

It cannot be said that the Soviet education system underestimates the importance of history; in fact, few education systems are more aware of the powerful influence history can

126

have on the minds of men. Specifically, the Soviet schools use history to show the superiority of the communistic system to that of any other system, past or present. A look at the curriculum and the history textbooks used in Soviet schools will suggest how thoroughly history is studied in order to strengthen the Communist world view.

Soviet students begin the formal study of history in the third grade inasmuch as a large section (about 20,000 words) of their third-grade reader is devoted to describing the major events of Russia's past. (See the table of contents at the end of Chapter 1.) Most of the selections in this part of the book are written in a straightforward expository style and include accounts of such major historical episodes and subjects as the early Slavs, the invasion of the Tatars, the Battle of Kulikovo, the war with the Swedes, the war of 1812, the 1905 uprising, the revolution of 1917, the five-year plans, the Second World War, and the postwar period, as well as accounts of historical figures such as Alexander Nevsky and Field Marshal Suvorov, and events such as the founding of Moscow and of St. Petersburg, the capture of Izmail, and the siege of Stalingrad. Some selections treat historical events in the form of a dramatic narrative, and there are poems by Pushkin, Nekrassov, and other poets celebrating historical events. Altogether there are forty-five selections carefully arranged in chronological order, from the beginning of Russian history to the present time.

In the fourth grade in Soviet schools, history becomes a separate subject and is taught with a separate textbook. This book is called *The History of the USSR* and consists of a 150-page account (about 27,000 words) of the history of Russia from its beginnings to the present. (See the table of contents at the end of this chapter.) From their readings in the third grade, Soviet students already have an acquaintance with the major events and some of the major figures in Russian history, but this fourth-grade book is a formal history written in a fairly formal expository style. It is somewhat simplified, but it is carefully written and it describes major historical events in a dramatic, even vivid manner.

Strict attention is paid to chronology, so that students grasp the continuity between what happened in the sixteenth and seventeenth centuries, and so on. This procedure is simply in accord with the realization that history means most to those who have a detailed knowledge of the sequence of events. Needless to say, the Communist view of history shows up in its worst and ugliest outlines in this book. But what needs to be stressed here is not the interpretation of history but the wealth of detail and the systematic presentation of it. As we shall see, it is not nearly so detailed as the Russian history that appears in the textbooks of the higher grades, but it is remarkable indeed for the fourth-grade level. Illustrations appear occasionally, but by no means as a substitute for text material; major battles are diagrammed; supplementary information is provided in captions beneath the illustrations, and questions for students to answer appear at the end of each subsection.

It can be said, then, that by the end of the fourth grade Soviet students are able to receive from their history textbooks a fairly detailed historical perspective of their country, even though the perspective is distorted, like the image in a funhouse mirror.

The history program in Soviet schools for the fifth through the tenth grades needs to be broadly described in order that its plan and scope may be understood. In general, the aim of the program is twofold. First, to give Soviet students a fairly detailed knowledge of the development of civilization, from prehistory to the present time. This preparation extends over a period of five years, from the fifth grade through the ninth. Second, to give students a thoroughly detailed study of Russia, from its historical origins to the present, over and above the training in history they have received in the third and fourth grades. This phase begins in the eighth grade and extends through the tenth. Thus in both the eighth and ninth grades,

Soviet students alternate semesters of world history with semesters of Russian history. But the main point to be made here is that Soviet students study history in each semester in every grade between the fourth and the tenth grades.

It was pointed out in the previous chapter that Soviet students are taught to read well enough by the end of the fourth grade so that in the fifth they can begin readings in literature at an adult level. The adult level is also maintained in their history readings. From the fifth grade on, their history books make almost no perceptible concessions, either in style or vocabulary, to the students' youthfulness. The style differs from that of a professional historian only in that the sentence structure may be simpler and the paragraphs shorter. The print in these history books is normal-sized, with normal line spacing. Illustrations, however, are sparse and crude, and the quality of the paper is terrible.

In the fifth grade and the first semester of the sixth grade, Soviet students study ancient history from a textbook entitled *History of the Ancient World.* (See the table of contents at the end of this chapter.) In the first semester of the fifth grade they acquire an amazingly detailed knowledge of ancient Egypt, the empire of Outer Asia and of Persia, of ancient India and ancient China. The account of ancient Egypt, for example, describes the people, the development of farming and handicrafts, the slaveholding system, the development of the Egyptian empire, the construction of the pyramids, scientific knowledge, and the Egyptian written language, the literature and art of ancient Egypt, and the fall of the Egyptian empire. The treatment of some of these topics is rather technical and detailed and is sometimes accompanied by illustrations. For example, a number of Egyptian hieroglyphics are reproduced alongside their Russian equivalents.

After thus studying the history of the ancient East in the first semester, fifth-grade Soviet students proceed to a study of the history of ancient Greece, to which they devote the whole second semester. They begin with a general account of the geography and population of ancient Greece, then proceed to an account of the Greek myths, with special attention to the story of the Trojan war and to Homer's *Odyssey*. This is followed by chapters on the Graeco-Persian wars, Greek culture, the Peloponnesian War, and the empire of Alexander the Great.

The detail in these chapters is often considerable. In the chapter called "The Growth of Culture in Greece," for example, there is a general account of the social and historical conditions which favor the development of culture in the Mediterranean area, an account of the origin and nature of the Olympic games, a description of the Greek theater, of the major Greek drama in general and of Sophocles' *Antigone* in particular, of Greek architecture and sculpture, including special discussions of the Acropolis, the Parthenon, the famous *Discobolus* of Myron (with an illustration), and the statuary of the Parthenon. The chapter concludes with a description of the learning and the schools of ancient Greece, heightened by an account of Herodotus' history of the Graeco-Persian wars and a summary statement of the significance of ancient Greek culture.

For their history lessons in the first semester of the sixth grade, Soviet students use the same texts as in the fifth, but they devote the entire semester to the study of ancient Rome. All the major historical events of the rise and fall of Rome are discussed and considerable attention is given to major historical figures. Here are a few of the more than 150 questions which appear in the chapters on Roman history, questions which all sixth-grade Soviet students are expected to be able to answer:

1. Indicate on the map the Tiber River, the City of Rome, and the location of the Latin settlements.

2. What events in Greece were taking place during the time the Roman Republic was being established?

3. What changes occurred in the government of Rome in the fifth to the third centuries before our era?

4. What were the causes of the First Punic War?

5. Indicate on the map the territory of the Roman Republic and the Carthaginian empire after the First Punic War.

6. Show on the map the locations of the chief battles during the time of the Second Punic War.

7. How did the Third Punic War differ basically from the first two?

8. What changes took place in the condition of the slaves from the sixth to the second century before our era?

9. How did Augustus concentrate the power of Rome into his own hands?

10. How did the changes in the Roman Army brought about by Marius prepare the way for the dictatorship of Sulla?

11. What innovations occurred in Roman architecture and sculpture?

12. When and why did Roman oratory begin to decline?

Beginning with the second half of the sixth grade, Soviet students are given a new history textbook called *History of the Middle Ages,* which they use until the end of the seventh grade. (See the table of contents at the end of this chapter.)

In the second semester of the sixth grade they read about the German and Slavic tribes, the fall of the Roman Empire, the establishment of the feudal system in Europe, the formation of the Frankish state, the Empire of Charlemagne, the establishment of the feudal system in the Byzantine and in Eastern Europe; the conquests of the Arabs, the collapse of the Arabian Caliphate, and the feudal system in India and China.

The seventh-grade history program devotes a whole year to a study of historical events occurring between 1150 and 1650.

In the textbook for this period, the history of every important European country is covered, in addition to various cultural developments, geographical discoveries, and technological advances; special attention is given to a host of major historical and cultural figures, such as Dante, Petrarch, Leonardo da Vinci, Raphael, Thomas More, Luther, Erasmus, Copernicus, Bruno, Galileo, Cervantes, and Shakespeare.

It can be seen, then, that Soviet students spend three years studying medieval and Renaissance history and that they do so with a remarkable degree of thoroughness.

As I have already indicated, Soviet students in the eighth and ninth grades study the history of the USSR in the first semester of each grade and world history in the second. The world-history textbook for the eighth and ninth grades is called *Novaya Isstoria* (New History, or Modern History) and is published in two volumes, one for each grade.

The volume for the eighth grade covers the period from 1650 to 1870. (See the table of contents at the end of this chapter.) The overwhelming emphasis, as might be expected, is on European history, especially the history of England, France, and Germany, though the history of India and China is not ignored, and American history is represented by two chapters. The second volume of *Novaya Isstoria,* used in the ninth-grade world-history course, covers the period from 1870 to the end of the First World War. The first chapter discusses the Franco-Prussian War and is followed by chapters on Germany, England, France, the United States, and China during that period. Also included are chapters on the International Workers Movement and one on international relations during that period. The textbook concludes with a long chapter on the First World War and an account of the October Revolution in Russia, which established communism as a form of government and as a way of life.

Soviet students round out their study of history in the high schools with a three-year program in the history of the USSR beginning in the eighth grade and ending in the tenth. Thus, in effect, they study the history of their own country in five different grades during their academic career: in the third grade, in the fourth grade, and again in a sequence of courses in the eighth, ninth, and tenth grades.

The textbook for the history of their own country in these upper grades is called simply the *History of the USSR*, and is in three volumes, one for each grade. Together these volumes total about 800 pages of normal-sized print—with a few illustrations—or about 260,000 words. In the eighth grade, Soviet students study the history of Russia from its beginnings to about 1750; in the ninth grade, from 1750 to about 1900; and in the tenth, from 1900 to the present. (See the table of contents for each grade at the end of this chapter.) It is important to note that these divisions in a general way parallel the Soviet student's study of the literature of his country, from grade to grade, so that his sense of history and of chronology is doubly strengthened.

From this review of the history program in Soviet schools it will be seen that Soviet students study history uninterruptedly from the latter part of the third grade through the tenth grade. They spend three and a third years studying the history of their own country, beginning in the latter part of the third grade, during all of the fourth grade, and concluding with a detailed study in the first semesters of the eighth and ninth grades and all of the tenth grade. In addition, they spend four years studying world history: ancient and medieval history in the fifth, sixth, and seventh grades, and modern history in the second semester of the eighth and ninth grades.

## HISTORY IN AMERICAN SCHOOLS

It is not so easy to describe the history program in American schools as in Soviet schools, because our program is not as standardized. Nevertheless, a curriculum pattern in most American schools is readily discernible, so that some valid and important generalizations can be made.

The status of history in American schools at the present time becomes clear only in the light of the development of what has come to be known as "the social studies," a concept which is now dominant both in the elementary and in the high schools in this country. Briefly, the social-studies concept was introduced in order to give students a better awareness of current social developments, and to emphasize the conditions of their own particular environment in their own time. The net effect of this concept has been to reduce the importance of a knowledge of history and of the past generally, and to stress the contemporaneous and the immediate. Furthermore, history, instead of remaining a separate subject taught every year, has become swallowed up in the social-studies programs and in some schools has now all but lost its identity. In its place a new emphasis is given to such courses as current events, civics, problems in democracy, contemporary problems, and courses which are simply called "social studies," and which, as we shall see, can include the study of almost anything.

One way of illustrating the decline of the teaching of history in American schools is to compare the recommendations of the Committee of Ten—which was appointed by the National Education Association and which was extremely influential in determining the curriculum of high schools during the first quarter of the century—with the recommendations of the Committee on Social Studies of the National Education Association, which were made in 1913.

The Committee of Ten in 1892 recommended a history program for the high schools as follows:

Grade  7:  American history and civil government
Grade  8:  Greek and Roman history
Grade  9:  French history, medieval and modern

Grade 10: English history, medieval and modern

Grade 11: American history

Grade 12: Intensive study of a special period, and civil government

> —Franklin Patterson, *High Schools for a Free Society*. The Free Press, Glencoe, Illinois, 1960, p. 36.

The Committee on Social Studies, however, wished to emphasize the social, civic, and political problems that are current at any given time, and therefore strongly de-emphasized the study of history. Their conclusions and recommendations have so won the day that in effect the history program in the majority of American high schools now follows this pattern:

Grade 7: History most often not taught at all

Grade 8: U. S. History

Grade 9: History most often not taught at all

Grade 10: World History

Grade 11: U. S. History

Grade 12: History most often not taught at all

> —Richard E. Gross and Leslie D. Zeleny, *Educating Citizens for Democracy*. Oxford University Press, New York, 1958, p. 70.

This tabulation does not mean, of course, that no students study history in the seventh, ninth, or twelfth grades. In the seventh grade, some study the history of the United States rather than geography, which is the social-studies subject most commonly offered; in the twelfth grade, some study the history of the United States rather than "contemporary problems," which is also most commonly taught; and a few may study state history in the ninth grade, where civics is most commonly taught. Nevertheless, as this table suggests, the majority of

135

American students study history during only three of their six years in junior high and senior high school, and only one of these years is devoted to history other than American history.

American history is, in fact, most frequently taught at intervals of three years, beginning with the fifth grade, so that students usually study it in the fifth, the eighth, and the eleventh grades. Thus students do, in fact, spend a sizable portion of their time studying American history, though the practice of offering it at wide intervals precludes the possibility of their studying it in anything like the detail that Soviet students study Russian history in the eighth, ninth, and tenth grades. Furthermore, although our students are thus given the opportunity to review what they have already learned, the three-year interval between courses creates a tendency to confuse what is new with what is review.

But as important as a good knowledge of American history is to all Americans, it in fact makes up only a small part, albeit an important part, of the history of the world. We may be reminded of how small a part it is by the fact that of the thirty-nine chapters in H. G. Wells' book *The Outline of History*, American history does not make its appearance until Chapter 35.

Yet, another glance at the table on page 135 will show that world history is studied for only one year in our high schools. Among notable exceptions are schools in Oregon and Wisconsin, where a two-year sequence of courses in world history in the ninth and tenth grades is offered. But it is quite possible that students may graduate from high school without studying world history at all, because sometimes modern history is offered instead; and where world history is an elective, a tenth-grade history course may be avoided altogether.

Many high school students do, however, get some sort of world-history course in the tenth grade. But it is a quickie course, a survey of history from Plato to the present, and the students move so fast from one civilization to another and one age to another that their heads are set aswim, and the historical knowledge they are able to pick up is necessarily both superficial and slight.

One widely used high school world-history text (*Story of Nations*), for example, explains the situation this way:

> In writing a textbook for high school students that will cover the whole span of world history, it is necessary to present only the high points—the mountain peaks of men's experiences. Many of the hills and valleys and waterfalls are pretty and interesting but they are likely to clutter up the landscape and confuse rather than enlighten the student. We have, therefore, tried to exclude everything that does not shed strong light on our story.

It would be highly desirable for students to know about the pretty valleys and waterfalls of history even at the risk of being confused, inasmuch as these might do much to enhance the students' interest in history. But as the above passage indicates, there is even less time and space for them than for many of the towering mountain peaks of man's experience which are also left out of this and similar world-history textbooks at the high school level.

Thus while Soviet students study world history systematically over a period of five years, American students try to do it in one year, and some, as we have seen, don't try it at all. The contrasts between the Soviet world-history program and the American program are bound to be sharp. For example, the American text called *Story of Nations*, which is widely used in *tenth*-grade world-history courses, devotes about 10,000 words to ancient Greek civilization as against 13,000 words in the *fifth*-grade Soviet history textbook. But even this disparity is minor compared to the respective treatment of the Middle Ages. *Story of Nations* has a section called "Europe During the Middle Ages," which covers the period from 700 A.D. to 1400 A.D. in less than 15,000 words as against the treatment of the same period in the sixth-grade Soviet history text which has 27,000 words, or nearly twice as much text. Nor does the *Story of Nations* compare favorably with regard to maps and illustrations. The American text for this section has 16 illustrations, none of them full-page illustrations, and only 3 maps; the corresponding section in the Soviet text has 42 illustrations, 7 of them full-page illustrations, and 21 maps.

Such comparisons between the Soviet history text and the *Story of Nations* or *Man's Story* or *World History* or *A History of the World* or any similar high school world-history texts may be multiplied endlessly. It should be pointed out, however, that these discrepancies are less reflections on world-history textbooks themselves than on a curriculum which permits only one year for the study of world history. Whereas Russian students devote a whole year to the ancient civilizations, American students devote little more than a month. An American student who had to stay home with a bad cold could miss out on Greek civilization, and if he happened to contract pneumonia he could miss out on the entire ancient world. But even if he hasn't missed a day, he is bound to come away from this one-year course with a knowledge of world history that is shallow and badly confused, as any history professor who teaches college freshmen will warmly testify.

American students also study history in elementary schools, usually beginning with the fourth grade, but again there is a serious problem in the curriculum. In the first place it should be noted that whereas in the Soviet schools students in every grade from the fourth through the ninth take courses in *both* history *and* geography, American elementary students as well as junior high and senior high students at any given time are studying *either* history *or* geography, and there are many times, especially under a social-studies program, when they are not studying either one. But even when they are studying history it is often difficult, in fact it is almost impossible, to detect any continuity or sequence of courses from grade to grade, for students may well be studying world history in one grade, for example, and American history or no history at all in the next.

A second problem in the teaching of history in the elementary grades is that textbooks now often attempt to correlate history and geography, so that both subjects are combined as a kind of historio-geography course. Under this program, the time devoted to this subject is not commonly doubled or even increased, and the textbooks themselves suggest that this procedure results in an ineffectiveness in the teaching of both.

The chief difficulty here is that history *must* be presented chronologically and that geography *cannot* be presented chronologically; therefore, to combine them means that one or the other of them must be presented illogically. In practice, however, a compromise is usually worked out, so that both are presented illogically, as the table of contents of this elementary "unified-studies" text called *Living Together in the Old World* will show:

Unit  1.   Our Earth
Unit  2.   How Early Man Lived and Learned
Unit  3.   The Countries of the Middle East
Unit  4.   The Countries of the Far East
Unit  5.   Greece and Its Neighbors
Unit  6.   Ancient Rome and Modern Italy
Unit  7.   Life in the Middle Ages
Unit  8.   Spain and Portugal
Unit  9.   France and the French Colonies
Unit 10.   Great Britain and the Commonwealth of Nations
Unit 11.   Belgium and the Netherlands
Unit 12.   Scandinavia and Finland
Unit 13.   Germany, a Great Industrial Nation
Unit 14.   The Countries of Central Europe
Unit 15.   The Union of the Soviet Socialist Republics
Unit 16.   The Continent of Africa
Unit 17.   Islands of the Pacific

Generally speaking, the organizational principle of this book appears in some way to accord with geographical areas, though some of the earlier units suggest that it is based upon historical periods. Although a sketch of the history of each country is given, it becomes extremely difficult for students to get any notion of what the sixteenth or the eighteenth century or any other century was like when history is thus presented. Furthermore, when spatial and time relationships are thus confused, the student cannot always be quite sure when he is studying geography and when he is studying history; it might be more accurate to say that he is studying a new subject which might be called "geostory" or "histraphy," or more accurately, a combination of these, "geohistoraphy." The disadvantages of such a text appear to far outweigh any possible advantages.

A third difficulty that textbooks present in the teaching of history in the elementary schools is that students who graduate from the third grade inherit a vocabulary of only about 1,000 words from their third-grade reader, so that unless they have learned to read from somewhere besides their readers, they tend to find the words in a good history book largely incomprehensible. As a result the choice is often whether to select a history textbook which children can understand but from which they cannot learn much history or a history text from which they can learn much history but which they cannot understand.

Still another threat to the teaching of history in the elementary schools, and also in the junior high schools, is a course entitled simply "social studies," which provides for the study of a great many things that have nothing to do with history. In practice, almost any subject can be, and often is, presented in the name of social studies. Samples of "units" or "projects," which have been recommended by social-studies experts or have actually been used in the classroom are the following: the value of part-time work; the need for self-analysis; vocational opportunities; plans for participation in tomorrow's world; buying insurance; planning a home; learning to play; the rise of typical American games; the postal service; theaters; movies; adjusting successfully to school; getting along better with people; the development of highways; the high school; the origin of social clubs and organizations; entering a new school; understanding myself and others; and vacation trips.

I have deliberately made this a long catalogue of possible social-studies topics, in order to suggest the limitless variety of subjects which are permitted to dwell under the social-studies roof. No one will deny that at least a few of these subjects are not without value, inasmuch as they may do something to adjust students to life, but it will be observed that neither these nor a host of other such subjects which stretch as far as the imagination can reach, have anything important to do with learning history.

All of these considerations lead to the conclusion that it would be extremely difficult to show that the history program in the vast majority of American schools, whether at the elementary, the junior high, or the senior high level, is at all adequate, and it would be even more difficult to show that it is not far weaker than that of the Soviet schools.

# Tables of Contents of Soviet History Textbooks

## FOURTH GRADE

*Title:* *History of the USSR*

*Chapter*

## FIFTH AND SIXTH GRADES

*Title:* *History of the Ancient World*

*Chapter*

VII: The Establishment of a Slaveholding System and the Formation of the State in Greece

VIII: The Graeco-Persian Wars and the Growth of Slavery in Greece

IX: The Growth of Culture in Greece

X: The Peloponnesian War and the Decline of Greece

XI: The Formation and Collapse of the Empire of Alexander the Great

XII: Formation of the Roman Slaveholding State and the Conquest of Italy

XIII: The Transformation of the Roman Republic into a Strong Mediterranean Empire. Further Growth of Slavery in Rome

XIV: Intensification of the Class Struggle in Rome in the Second Half of the Second Century B.C.

XV: The Fall of the Roman Republic. The Roman Empire in the Period of Its Power

## SIXTH AND SEVENTH GRADES

*Title: History of the Middle Ages*

### I: THE DEVELOPMENT OF THE FEUDAL COUNTRIES

*Chapter*

I: The Germans and the Slavs. The Fall of the Western Roman Empire

II: The Eastern Roman Empire and the Slavs

III: The Establishment of the Feudal System in Europe

IV: The Establishment of the Feudal System in the East

143

## II:  THE STRENGTH AND FURTHER DEVELOPMENT OF THE FEUDAL SYSTEM. THE FORMATION OF THE CENTRAL STATES

I: The Development of Handicrafts and Trade. The Growth of the Cities

II: The Crusades

III: The Mongol Invasion

IV: The Formation of the Central States in Europe

V: The Attack on the German Feudal Lords in the East and Their Fall

VI: The Struggle Against the German Forces and the Peasant's War in Czechoslovakia

VII: The Turkish Conquests

VIII: The Culture of Western Europe in the Twelfth and Thirteenth Centuries

IX: The Origin of the Bourgeoisie and Bourgeois Culture

## III:  THE BEGINNING OF THE DECAY OF FEUDALISM AND THE ORIGIN OF CAPITALISTIC ATTITUDES

I: Geographical Discoveries at the End of the Fifteenth and the Beginning of the Sixteenth Centuries

II: The Reformation and the Peasants' War in Germany

III: Absolute Monarchy in France

IV: England in the Sixteenth Century and the Beginning of the Seventeenth Century

V: The Netherland Bourgeois Revolution

VI: Eastern Europe in the Sixteenth and First Half of the Seventeenth Century

VII: China in the Fourteenth–Seventeenth Centuries

VIII: The Development of Technology, Science, and Art in the Sixteenth and First Half of the Seventeenth Century

144

# EIGHTH GRADE

*Title: Modern History* (Part I)

## I: THE BEGINNINGS OF MODERN TIMES

*Chapter*

  I: The English Bourgeois Revolution in the Seventeenth Century
 II: The Enslavement of English India. The Beginning of the Industrial Revolution in England
III: The War for Independence in North America
 IV: The Feudal Structure in European Mainland Countries

## II: EUROPE AT THE END OF THE EIGHTEENTH CENTURY AND THE BEGINNING OF THE NINETEENTH CENTURY

  V: The French Bourgeois Revolution of the Eighteenth Century
 VI: Europe from 1794 to 1815

## III: FROM THE CONGRESS OF VIENNA TO THE REVOLUTION OF 1848

 VII: The Congress of Vienna. The Holy Alliance. The Revolutionary Movement of the First Twenty Years of the Nineteenth Century
VIII: France from 1815 to 1848
 IX: England from 1815 to 1848
  X: Utopian Socialism (Saint-Simon, Fourier, Owen)
 XI: The Rise of Scientific Communism—Karl Marx and F. Engels

XII: The Revolution of 1848 in France

XIII: The Revolution of 1848 in Germany

XIV: The Revolution of 1848 in the Nations of the Austrian Empire

### IV: THE FIFTIES AND SIXTIES OF THE NINETEENTH CENTURY

XV: The Crimean War. England and India in the Fifties and Sixties of the Nineteenth Century

XVI: The Civil War in North America

XVII: China in the Seventeenth–Nineteenth Centuries

XVIII: The Unification of Italy

XIX: The Unification of Germany

XX: The First International from Its Origins to 1870

XXI: The Basic Result of the First Period of Modern History

## EIGHTH GRADE

*Title: History of the USSR* (Part I)

### I: THE PRIMITIVE SOCIAL AND SLAVEHOLDING STRUCTURE. THE SLAVS IN ANTIQUITY

*Chapter*

I: The Primitive Social Structure in the Territories of Our Country

II: Slaveholding Structure in the Southern Territories of Our Country

III: The Eastern Slavs in Antiquity

XII: Economic and Political Development of Russia in the Seventeenth Century

XIII: The War of Liberation of the Ukraine and White Russian People

XIV: The People's Russia in the Second Half of the Seventeenth Century. The Peasants' War, 1667-1671

XV: Russian Culture in the Seventeenth Century

# NINTH GRADE

*Title: Modern History* (Part II)

*Chapter*

I: The Franco-Prussian War. The Paris Commune.

II: Germany at the End of the Nineteenth Century and the Beginning of the Twentieth Century

III: England at the End of the Nineteenth and the Beginning of the Twentieth Century

IV: France at the End of the Nineteenth and the Beginning of the Twentieth Century

V: The South and West Slavs in the Seventies of the Nineteenth Century

VI: The United States of America at the End of the Nineteenth Century and the Beginning of the Twentieth

VII: China at the End of the Nineteenth and Beginning of the Twentieth Century

VIII: International Workers Movement and the Second International

IX: Imperialism as the Highest and Last Stage of Capitalism

X: International Relations at the End of the Nineteenth and the Beginning of the Twentieth Century

XI: The First World War, 1914-1918

*Title: History of the USSR* (Part II)

### I: THE RUSSIAN NOBLES' EMPIRE
### IN THE EIGHTEENTH CENTURY

*Chapter*

  i: The Formation of the Russian Empire
 ii: The Russian Empire under the Successors of Peter I (1725-1762)
iii: The Nobles' Empire, the Second Half of the Eighteenth Century

### II: THE DECAY OF SERFDOM AND
### THE ORIGIN OF CAPITALISM

 iv: Czarism at the End of the Eighteenth Century and Its Struggle with the French Bourgeois Revolution of 1789
  v: The Great Patriotic War of 1812. The Defeat of Napoleon
 vi: The People of Czarist Russia and Colonial Politics of Czarism in the First Quarter of the Nineteenth Century
vii: The Decembrists
viii: Crisis of the Feudal System
 ix: Czarism—The Gendarme of Europe
  x: Social Movements and the Culture of Russia in the Thirties to the Fifties of the Nineteenth Century
 xi: Bourgeois Reforms of the 1860's
xii: The Development of Capitalism in the Sixties and Seventies
xiii: The Beginning of the Struggle of the Working Class Against Czarism (1881-1899)

## TENTH GRADE

*Title: History of the USSR* (Part III)

### I:   THE PERIOD OF IMPERIALISM.
### THE BOURGEOIS DEMOCRATIC
### REVOLUTION IN RUSSIA

*Chapter*

  I:   The Eve of the First Russian Revolution
  II:   The Russo-Japanese War. The Revolution of 1905-1907 in Russia. The First People's Revolution of the Era of Imperialism
  III:   Russia in the Period of Reaction (1907-1911)
  IV:   New Advances of the Worker Movement (1910-1914)
  V:   Russia in the First World War. The February Bourgeois Democratic Revolution
  VI:   The Preparation for the Great October Socialist Revolution
  VII:   The Victory of the Great October Socialist Revolution
  VIII:   The Struggle for the Consolidation of Soviet Rule

### II:   FOREIGN WARS OF INTERVENTION
### AND THE CIVIL WAR (1918-1920)

  IX:   The Beginning of the War of Intervention and Civil War
  X:   The Defeat of the Three Campaigns of the Entente

### III:   THE RECONSTRUCTION OF THE
### PEOPLE'S ECONOMY. THE STRENGTHENING
### OF THE MULTI-NATION SOVIET STATE
### (1921-1925)

  XI:   The Progress in the Peaceful Work Toward the Construction of the People's Economy

# 5

## GEOGRAPHY
## IN SOVIET AND AMERICAN
## SCHOOLS

A solid knowledge of geography is most often valued not for itself but for its vital relationship to other branches of knowledge. It is essential, for example, to an understanding of history, economics, political science, military science, sociology, archeology, meteorology, seismology, and a host of other important areas of inquiry. In fact, without a sound knowledge of geography, learned men and specialists would not be able to carry on either practical or theoretical work in these and other major fields. But apart from such practical and obvious instances of the importance of knowing geography, it is primarily upon his knowledge of geography that anyone depends in orienting himself, his community, and his country to the rest of the world. The study of history or literature or current events does not help him much in this orientation, and the study of most other subjects does not help at all. For these reasons, it is mandatory that geography be well taught in American schools.

Yet, it is a common observation that one of the most neglected of all the basic subjects in American schools is geography. This chapter will suggest that there are very good reasons for believing that it is badly neglected; it will also suggest that there are very good reasons for believing that the Soviet school system does not neglect it. It might almost be said, in fact, that the Soviet schools have a passion for geography.

The curriculum of the Soviet school system calls for six years of geography, beginning in the fourth grade and continuing uninterruptedly through the ninth. During the first four years Soviet students study various aspects of physical and political geography, and in the eighth and ninth grades they study economic geography.

Even in the third grade, Soviet students are introduced to some basic geographical facts through their reader, which has a large section called "Geography and Natural Science." From this section they learn something about how to make and read maps, how to tell directions, how to read a barometer, and something about such phenomena as the winds, the weather, and the apparent motion of the sun. (See page 44.)

In the fourth grade, geography is taught more systematically and from a separate geography textbook. In the early chapters of this book Soviet students learn more about reading maps and they become acquainted with the continents and oceans of the world. Most of the work in geography in this grade, however, deals with the geography of the USSR. (See the table of contents at the end of this chapter.) Students learn about the seas and lakes and rivers and mountain ranges of the Soviet Union; about its natural geographic zones such as the tundra, the taiga, the steppes, and the wastes; about such geographical regions as the Urals and the Caucasus; about some of the major republics of the USSR; and about the city of Moscow. Some of the material is presented in narrative or anecdotal form, but the selections are rather carefully written and often highly informative.

The fifth-grade geography textbook provides students with

more detailed information about the physical features of the
earth. (See the table of contents at the end of this chapter.)
They learn still more about maps and kinds of maps, and about
various kinds of dry-land surfaces and bodies of water. They
learn about the movement of the sun and earth, about weather
and the instruments for measuring weather, about climate and
its relation to living things, and about population and the
various races of the earth. The style in this textbook is entirely
expository and businesslike, for as we have seen, by the fifth
grade Soviet students are expected to be able to read well.

The sixth-grade geography text discusses the continents of
the world in some detail, and in systematic fashion. (See the
table of contents at the end of this chapter.) First the location
and boundaries of each continent are described, then the characteristics of the land and water surfaces and natural zones are
indicated, and then the geographical features of the major
countries and cities of each continent are discussed. Forty-five
pages, for example, are devoted to the section called "America."
These include a 3-page description of the land mass of North
and South America; a one-page account of Columbus' discovery
of America; a 2-page account of the general features of North
America; a 4-page discussion of the climate of North America,
with the aid of four maps and numerous statistics; and a 3-page
discussion of the natural geographical zones, with more maps
and pictures. After a similar treatment of the geography of
South America, the section concludes with a 7-page discussion
of the population and political boundaries of North and South
America.

The seventh-grade geography textbook used in Soviet schools
treats the physical geography of the USSR, but this time in
more detail than the fourth-grade geography text. (See the
table of contents at the end of this chapter.) The first half of
the book is a general survey of the geography of the USSR and
consists of five- to ten-page discussions of the borders, the seas,
the terrain, the climate, the internal bodies of water, the natu-

ral geographic zones, the political divisions, and the national economy of the USSR. The second part describes the geography of the individual republics of the USSR.

The curriculum in the Soviet schools places great emphasis upon economic geography, and Soviet students study it in both the eighth and ninth grades. The eighth-grade course deals with the economic geography of foreign countries, and the ninth-grade course is concerned with the economic geography of the USSR. The textbooks for both courses are large and extremely detailed, and, of course, include a great deal of physical and political geography also.

In the eighth-grade text the economic geography of the major foreign countries is treated at length. (See the table of contents at the end of this chapter.) The United States and China, for example, are covered in 22 pages each, Great Britain in 18 pages, and India in 13 pages. But every small country that has any economic significance at all is also discussed. For example, Iran gets 6 pages, Pakistan, Vietnam, and Indonesia each get 4 pages, and Iceland, Portugal, and Luxemburg get one apiece. Generally speaking, each country is described according to its general geographical conditions, its population, its industry and agriculture, its cities, and its governmental structure. Statistical data are furnished at every turn.

The ninth-grade geography text, a 340-page book with rather closely printed pages, treats the economic geography of the USSR in considerable detail. (See the table of contents at the end of this chapter.) The first half of the book discusses the characteristics of the national economy, the geography of heavy industry, of light industry, of the rural economy, and of transportation. The second part consists of a survey of the various republics and regions of the USSR.

Even in so objective a study as geography, Soviet textbooks overlook no opportunity for Communist indoctrination, not principally by altering geographical facts, but, as the concluding chapter of this book will indicate, by the interpretation of them. Nevertheless, it will be seen that the geography program in Soviet schools is a strong one indeed.

The strongest feature of the program lies in the fact that Soviet students study geography continuously for a period of six years. At no time from the fourth through the ninth grades are they not studying it. There is a tendency for the geography text of one grade to review material of a previous grade and at the same time to present new and more detailed material, so that the amount of geography taught in the eighth and ninth grades is very substantial indeed.

But apart from the curriculum, there are certain features of the textbooks themselves which contribute immensely to the effective teaching of geography. The most important of these is that the material is presented in highly systematic fashion. The principle here is that students should learn, first, all the most important geographical facts and should then proceed to learn the more dependent and detailed facts. Thus Soviet students learn first about the continents in general, then the various countries, and then the cities. Or, in learning about the climate or the surface characteristics of a geographical area, they proceed from the general to the particular, so that no basic facts are omitted and so that more detailed geographical facts are seen in their proper perspective. As the last chapter indicated, basic geographical information cannot be presented in chronological order but only in logical—or illogical—order. The effective teaching of geography depends heavily upon a logical and systematic presentation of it. Even a glance at the table of contents of the Soviet geographies as they are reprinted at the end of this chapter will suggest that the presentation is logical and systematic indeed.

Another important feature of Soviet geographies is the heavy reliance upon maps. A map is worth almost as many words as a picture, particularly to a student who is learning geography. It is all well and good to have large classroom maps for common use, and many Soviet classrooms have such maps, but for either class work or homework there is no substitute for a student having his own maps. Certainly Soviet geography textbooks reflect the realization that very little geography can be learned without maps, and special care is taken to see that students have ready access to their own private maps. Each geography textbook has a map supplement in loose-leaf form. These maps are all in color and are of various sizes, depending upon their purpose. In addition, however, the pages of the geography texts beginning with the sixth grade are liberally sprinkled with black and white maps of all sorts and sizes. For example, the sixth-grade textbook, in addition to the 12-map supplement, has 55 black and white maps scattered throughout its pages; the seventh-grade text has 12 color maps and 23 black and white maps; the eighth-grade economic-geography text has 17 color maps and 74 maps in black and white, and the ninth-grade text, which deals with the economic geography of the USSR, has 116 black and white maps.

Still another feature that makes the teaching of geography effective in Soviet schools is that, since most students are expected to be able to read well by the end of the fourth grade, few concessions need be made in the matter of vocabulary in the geography texts; therefore the style, though not very often exciting, is mature and extremely informational.

How, then, does the geography program in American schools compare with that in Soviet schools with regard, first, to curriculum, and second, to textbooks?

The social-studies program, which is largely peculiar to the American school system, has done perhaps even more harm to the geography curriculum than to the history curriculum. As we have seen, social-studies programs leave semesters and even entire school years during which students do not study history at all. The social-studies programs allow even more semesters and years during which students do not study geography.

The social-studies curriculum varies somewhat from system to system at all grade levels, so that one cannot say that geography is or is not taught at any given grade level. But it is possible to state with a fairly high degree of accuracy the total number of semesters or years that students spend studying geography during their school days. And unfortunately the total is not very large.

Generally speaking, geography is not taught systematically after the seventh grade, except sometimes as an elective course in high school, where it is studied by approximately 7 per cent of the students. Similarly, it is ordinarily not taught systematically before the fourth grade since, unlike Soviet third-grade readers, American third-grade readers usually tell students nothing about geography. Many American students do in fact study geography in the seventh grade, though they may do so from a "unified social-studies" textbook which, as we saw in the last chapter, attempts to combine geography and history. Also, somewhere between the fourth and the sixth grades all students are certain to get some training in geography, though it is unlikely to be a separate course taught during the same term as history, as in the Soviet schools. Rather, it has to compete with history in these grades, and is either alternated with semesters of history or mingled with it in a historio-geography course. In some schools it may also compete with other social-studies subjects or "units" which have nothing important to do with either history or geography. Thus, American students do not generally spend more than a year and a half on geography in the elementary grades and they may spend less. This year and a half of elementary school geography added to the year that most students study geography in the seventh grade totals two and a half years for most American students, as against six years for Soviet students.

What, then, are our children able to learn from their textbooks during the few years in which they study geography? Fortunately, there is a considerably wider range in the quality of basal-geography textbooks available to our schools than of basal readers, and a few in fact do present geography systematically, thoroughly, effectively and interestingly. I wish here, however, to dwell upon certain features of some basal geographies which appear to seriously impede students in their attempt to acquire a good knowledge of geography during the short time that they study it.

One of these difficulties is the practice of "unified-studies" textbooks to attempt to combine history and geography, a practice which, as has been stressed, necessarily reduces the effectiveness of learning both history and geography, because it prevents the systematic presentation of either subject and because it provides for serious gaps in the presentation of both.

But even in textbooks in which geography does not have to compete with history, the presentation of the material is often still illogical. Some textbooks, for example, sacrifice a presentation of basic geographical information in order to concentrate upon a few countries which have widely varying geographical conditions. This kind of geography is perhaps best described as "sample geography." A typical elementary geography text entitled *Our Big World* will illustrate the "sample-geography" approach. It contains chapters on the following countries: Iceland, Norway, Holland, Switzerland, Greece, Egypt, the Congo, Australia, the Philippines, and the China Coast; and a chapter called "Alaska to Cape Horn," which touches on Alaska, California, Ecuador, Peru, and Chile. In such a geography, most of the basic geographical facts of the world are necessarily ignored, and many of the most important countries and areas of the world are not even mentioned.

But even the organizational principle of a geography of this sort may have some, though not much, justification. Other geographies used in the elementary grades are based upon an organizational principle that is patently false. In the Foreword to another elementary school geography, called *Journey through Many Lands*, there appears, for example, the statement that an understanding of geography is "especially dependent" upon an understanding of the various means of transportation. An understanding of geography is, of course, far more dependent upon other things than modes of travel, but this principle lends support to the presentation of a particular kind of geography, which is, in fact, commonly described as "journey geography." The idea here is that a student will become more interested in geography if he imagines himself or some other child taking a trip through the lands that are discussed in his geography book. Geography thus takes on the character of a story, which in theory at least might do something to interest students who otherwise might not be interested. In practice, however, this "journey-geography" or you-are-there geography is often coupled with "sample geography," so that many texts thus combine the bad features of both, i.e., an incomplete coverage of basic geographical information and a highly inefficient presentation of geography as a result of glossing over in the narrative the few facts that are presented.

The elementary geography, *Journeys through Many Lands,* for instance, has a chapter entitled "Across the United States on the Lincoln Highway." In the course of the ensuing automobile trip, the students visit New York City, Philadelphia, Pittsburgh, Chicago, Omaha (with a side trip to Yellowstone Park), Salt Lake City, Sacramento, and San Francisco. The chief difficulty is that any region or state or city that is not on or near the Lincoln Highway does not have much of a chance —except Yellowstone Park. The fact that this book also has chapters on the Congo, Egypt, Holland, Switzerland, and Norway, but does not even mention England, Germany, or Russia, suggests how shamelessly the geography textbooks tend to imitate one another.

Another elementary school geography, called *My World of Neighbors,* proceeding on the same principles of "sample geography" combined with "journey geography," begins with Peter and Dad preparing for a long trip. The reader by this time can without difficulty imagine what countries Peter and Dad visit: Brazil, Holland, Switzerland, Egypt and, not the Congo this time, but Uganda. Dad and Peter never get to France or Germany or England or Russia, or to most of the other important countries in the world. First, however, Peter and Dad must cross the United States. Since Dad works for an airline they go by plane rather than by car, but they nonetheless fly along the route of the Lincoln Highway, and they land at—let the reader guess, if he will let his memory work in reverse—Salt Lake City (with an inevitable side trip to Yellowstone Park), Omaha, Chicago, Pittsburgh, not Philadelphia this time but Washington, D.C., and New York.

"Lincoln-Highway" geography appears to be a solidly established tradition among American geographies in the elementary grades. The second chapter of another of these geographies, *Our Neighbors Near and Far,* is entitled "We Cross Our Own United States." "We" of course cross it by way of the Lincoln Highway, following the same route as the other "journey geographies," including the side trip to Yellowstone Park. It is as if these geographies were in competition with one another to see which could present the least geography. They are all strong candidates for the winner.

But there is even a worse kind of geography than these, for sometimes the story element in these elementary geographies so far gets the upper hand that the author forgets to present any geography at all. One of these, which belongs to the "unified-studies" species and is called *Friends Near and Far,* will illustrate this difficulty. The foreword to this book says that "each unit consists of a well-written story, with a plot centering around a particular family and their friends and neighbors." A sample from Unit I, entitled "Pimwe, Jungle Boy," will give the reader an idea of what American geography texts can be like:

> Pimwe looked up into the treetops. He could see them swaying with the wind. The sky was growing darker. He knew that the afternoon rain was coming.
> Suddenly it started to pour. But they kept walking through the

jungle. They had no clothing to get soaked. They knew the rain soon would stop.

After the rain, the whole forest was soaking wet. So was every plant and animal in it. The monkeys shook themselves to get rid of the water. The butterflies were so wet they could hardly fly. For several minutes afterward little showers fell from every overhanging branch.

"Come along," Pika called to the boys. "We must find the trap."

Pimwe darted ahead of the others. He was anxious to know what was in the trap. Soon he called back. "Father, the trap is empty." Pimwe was disappointed. He had hoped to find a wild pig, or at least a squirrel.

Pika was disappointed too. "I was afraid it would be like that. The animals are moving farther into the forest. They do not like the neighborhood of our village. This trap has been here for several days. If any animals still roamed this part of the forest, we should have caught one."

"But how can I learn to hunt and be a man if there are no animals?" Bua asked.

Pimwe and Pika laughed. "That is right. It does not do much good to be a clever hunter if you have nothing to hunt," said Pika.

"And how shall I ever kill my first deer?" asked Pimwe.

When they gathered around the fire for supper that evening, Topo looked at Pimwe. "Couldn't you find the deer you were going to kill?"

"No, Mother. We did not find anything. Even in the trap there was nothing. My brother will never learn to hunt if he sees only shadows and tapir tracks."

"That is right. Food is growing scarce around here. I heard your uncles say that the chief is calling a meeting of all the men. It will be tomorrow. Many people think we should move the village to a place where there is more food."

"That is good," said Pika. "My brothers and I shall meet with the chief. We shall then decide what is best to do."

This sort of geography might be described as "anonymous geography" or "guess-where?" geography, because the student is never told where Pimwe lives. If he is observant, however,

162

he will find hints such as occasional mention of the Amazon River and a strip map of the Amazon River, which together with the mention of "Brazil nuts" may lead him to the conclusion that Pimwe lives in Brazil, provided that he knows there is such a country as Brazil. Another unit in this book is about José, who lives somewhere in Central America, but the only place even this information is obtainable is in one of the captions under an illustration. Another unit tells a story about Tommy, who lives in Milltown, which is somewhere in the Midwestern part of the United States; and another is about Joe Many Goats, who lives in the Southwest. There are also stories about Chris, who apparently lives somewhere in Scandinavia, and about Nancy in Eskimo land.

It must be said that the authors of this book protect themselves by not calling it a geography. In fact, in the Foreword is the observation that "Much of it might well be classified as elementary sociology. Geography, history, science, art, music, and other subjects have been woven together into one unified whole." The Foreword doesn't say what it is a "whole" of, and it is difficult to know what subject the book is about, since the students who use it can't learn any more about sociology, history, science, art, music, or any other subject than they can about geography. It might, of course, make a good story book, were it not for the fact that it is badly written.

Perhaps one of the best ways of illustrating the virtues and defects of both the American and Soviet geography textbooks is to place side by side their respective treatments of a single country. Following is a sample of how a typical seventh-grade American textbook of the "journey-geography" type treats the subject of Denmark and of how the Soviet eighth-grade geography treats it. A seventh-grade American text is perhaps best chosen here because American students do not normally study geography after the seventh grade; and an eighth-grade Soviet text is best chosen because in the seventh grade Soviet students study the geography of the USSR rather than of the world.

# What Ivan Knows That Johnny Doesn't

## From *Exploring the Old World*

### *Denmark Grows Breakfast for Europe*

All about is the hustle of the busy harbor of Copenhagen (ko′ pen ha′ gen), the capital of Denmark. Small fishing boats go chugging by. A ferryboat, loaded with people and cars, heads for Sweden, a few miles away. A long blast comes from an ocean liner bound for America.

Even before we land, we hear the noise of the city—the clatter of great cranes unloading ships, the honking of auto horns, and the shrill whistles of factories.

Copenhagen is the heart of Denmark. Nearly 800,000 people live in this great port city. It is the manufacturing, trading, and cultural center of the country.

Our ship nudges the dock, the gangplank goes down, and we hurry ashore. A friendly customs official inspects our passports and wishes us a pleasant stay in Denmark.

*Beautiful Copenhagen.* We spend our first day sight-seeing in Copenhagen. When we return to our hotel, we talk over the many interesting sights we have seen.

"What did you like most about Copenhagen?" asks Mrs. Gray.

"Oh, the beautiful parks with their statues and fountains," answers Sue.

"The stores," says Fred. "The department stores here look just like ours at home."

"I liked the trip through the big diesel factory," adds Tony, "but I thought the restaurant where we had lunch was the most interesting place of all. Boy, I have never seen such a big menu! It was four feet long and had over 500 different items on it."

"I was impressed by the number of bookstores we saw," says Mr. Gray. "It must be true that the Scandinavian people get a good education."

"I'll tell you what I liked best," says Peggy. "The people! Everyone tried to help us. And do you remember the thousands of people going home from work on their bicycles? Did you ever see so many cheerful faces? That's what I liked best."

*Denmark is a tiny country.* It is made up of a small peninsula and many scattered islands. Much of the land is low, rolling plains. Unlike the other Scandinavian countries, Denmark has no mountains and has few forests.

*A land of many factories.* Most of Denmark's factories process foods such as butter, cheese, meats, and sugar. Her other important factories make cloth, chemicals, and machinery.

*Visiting a farm family.* The next morning we drive through a gently rolling countryside, past fields of potatoes, sugar beets, wheat, and other grain. We turn off the blacktop road and stop beside a white farmhouse with a neat lawn and beds of petunias and geraniums.

Two things catch our eye—the red-and-white flag of Denmark flying from a pole and the whole family dressed in their Sunday best, standing ready to greet us.

"Welcome to our farm," a tall blond boy says, as we step from the car. "This is my family—my father and mother, Mr. and Mrs. Karl Pedersen, my brother Erik, and my sister Karen. My name is Chris. I learned English in high school."

Erik says something in Danish. "He wants you to know that this is his birthday," says Chris. "That's why the flag is flying."

Later, Mrs. Pedersen shows us through the home. Pictures of the family hang on the walls, and potted plants bloom in the window sills. Mrs. Pedersen is proud of her kitchen, with its electric stove and new refrigerator.

*A land where pigs, cows, and chickens are very important.* "Now would you like to see our farm?" asks Chris. We walk across the courtyard to a new brick barn. Inside is a long row of pens filled with squealing pigs. "They think we have come to feed them," says Chris, as he scratches one of the pigs behind the ear.

Next we walk through the well-scrubbed dairy barn. A long line of red cows stand munching sweet-scented hay. "We also have chickens," Chris tells us. "Bacon, butter, and eggs are important products of Danish farms."

"Who eats all the bacon, butter, and eggs?" asks Fred.

"You probably ate some for breakfast when you were in the British Isles and Germany," answers Chris. "In return for our foods, we get steel, coal, iron goods, and cotton and other textiles.

So you see why it is so important for Danish farmers to take good care of their land, use large amounts of fertilizer, and grow big crops."

From the Soviet Eighth-Grade Geography Text:
*Economic Geography of Foreign Countries—Denmark*

Area, 43,000 square kilometers; Population, 4.4 Million
Constitutional Monarchy. Capital—Copenhagen

*Geographical conditions.* Denmark is located between the Baltic and the North Seas. It occupies a large part of the Jutland Peninsula and the group of neighboring islands, the most important of these being Sealand and Fyn. Its only dry-land border is in the South with the Federation of German Republics; on the north its nearest neighbors are the countries of the Scandinavian peninsulas—Sweden and Norway—from which it is divided by narrow straits (see the map), through which runs an important seaway from the Baltic to the North Sea.

On the Baltic Sea the island of Bornholm belongs to Denmark and in the Atlantic Ocean the Faeroes Islands. Also Denmark owns the largest island in the world—Greenland (see map).

*Natural conditions.* Denmark is a maritime country. The sea has had a great influence upon its nature and its economy. The eastern shores of Jutland and the shores of the islands have sharp divisions, thanks to which they have many coves and natural fiords, favorable to the early development of maritime and fishing industries. As to the structure of the land surface of Denmark, it differs from the other European countries in that it consists of gently rolling lowlands, formed by deposits of former ice-floes which occurred ten or twelve thousand years ago. In the region of this country there is not a single significant elevation.

The climate formed under the influence of warm west winds is maritime and damp. The mean temperature for July is 19° (centigrade), for January it is about 0° (centigrade). The precipitation is relatively evenly distributed during the course of the year.

The soil (in the east it is clayey, in the west sandy and swampy) demands the application of fertilizer and careful cultivation.

Three-quarters of the territory of the country is used for agriculture, the rest consists of small forests, wastes, sand dunes, and swamps. The climatic and soil conditions are more favorable for the cultivation of grasses and forage-cap, which comprise the food base for livestock.

*Useful Minerals.* Denmark does not have the important minerals —coal, oil, iron ore, and the ore of colored metals. All these it must import from abroad. Its mineral resources consist of layers of porcelain-clay and a small quantity of peat. Recently a large salt deposit has been discovered.

*Population.* The Danes by virtue of their language and culture are related to the Scandinavian people—the Swedes and Norwegians. A large part of the population lives on islands (the mean density on the island of Zealand is 240 men per square kilometer). The population of the Jutland peninsula is significantly less dense. Here the population is predominantly in the city. There have been many seamen among the Danes. Some of them reached the shores of America earlier than Columbus. The fairy tales of the Danish writer Anderson are widely known.

*Agriculture.* The basis of the agriculture consists in the large quantities of meat and dairy products from poultry and cattle raising. The products from such livestock are fresh butter, bacon, eggs, and cheese exported to England, West Germany, and other European countries. Agriculture serves chiefly for cattle raising. Grasses, beets for fodder, turnips, oats, and barley are raised. Part of the feed is imported from abroad. As in cattle raising, so also in agriculture, reigning conditions belong to an economy of the capitalistic type in which machines are used, mineral fertilizer, and the widespread use of hired workers for agricultural work. The financing and control by the banks has an important significance for the agricultural farms with feed, fertilizer, and machines. By means of the co-operatives, they conduct the wholesaling of agricultural products for foreign and domestic markets.

*Industry.* Industry yields more than one-third of the national income. The branches of heavy industry (metalworking, shipbuilding, agricultural machinery) and also the textile industry operate with imported raw materials. These are distributed in the maritime port cities. The branches of the food industry (dairy, butter products, and tinned meat products) are prepared from their own agriculture products and are distributed throughout the country. A prominent place in the country is occupied by navigation and fishing.

*Cities.* Copenhagen (1.2 million inhabitants), the capital and chief industrial center and port of Denmark, is one of the oldest cities in Europe. It has important shipyards and plants for the manufacturing of machinery. The food industry is growing. Various textile goods are made there and shoes, jewelry, and porcelain manufacture. Danish porcelain ware is highly valued abroad.

The virtues and defects of both the American and Soviet geographies are to a degree represented in these passages. There can be no doubt that the treatment of Denmark in the American textbook would have a greater appeal for some students. Futhermore, the American account is calculated to instill in students a friendly attitude toward Denmark, whereas the Soviet presentation does not have that effect.

On the other hand, there seems also to be no doubt that the Soviet version furnishes far more geographical information about Denmark, that it does so in a far more systematic manner, and in a prose style that is not deliberately oversimplified. The presentation of geographical information in the American version is not only disorganized and chaotic but is so watered down that if a few sentences and a few words were deleted the rest might be equally descriptive of a dozen European countries and a hundred European cities anywhere in Europe. Given the obvious severe limitations of both methods of presentation, the question still remains, which serves to inform its students better, for presumably the chief reason for studying geography is to learn geography.

I would emphasize again that not all American geographies on the market are bad, but the fact that the bad geographies far outnumber the good ones certainly suggests that bad geographies are more widely used in our schools. Needless to say, in such vital aspects of geography as instruction in map reading, bad American geographies make a very poor showing indeed compared to Soviet geographies, not only in the explanation of the principles and the kinds of maps, but in exercises in reading maps.

In terms of quality, the maps that appear in American geographies are, by and large, far superior to those in Soviet geographies. Color maps in American geographies are often as fine as one could hope for. Some American texts, however, leave much to be desired in the way of large-scale maps of individual countries or small but important geographical areas, and often they are not sufficiently detailed or in sufficient number. Few of the junior high school geographies that I have seen come close in either the number (see page 157 above) or the kinds of maps that appear in the eighth- or ninth-grade Soviet geographies, or in the number of times in which students are invited to consult their maps. Each of the 50 sections in the Soviet sixth-grade geography book, for example, begins with rather extensive exercises, under the heading "Map Work."

How much our students are able to learn about geography over and above what they learn in the short time they spend studying it in school and with the handicap of poor textbooks, is not easily measurable, but the reflection that our students probably spend only two and a half years or less studying geography and studying it from bad textbooks and that Soviet students spend six years studying geography from thorough and mature and carefully written textbooks appears to leave little doubt as to which students learn more geography.

# Tables of Contents of Soviet Geography Textbooks

*(In Shortened Form)*

## FOURTH GRADE

*Title: Geography of the USSR*

*Chapter*

    I: Understanding Diagrams
    II: The Globe
    III: The Seas of the USSR
    IV: The Plains and Mountains of the USSR
    V: The Great Rivers and Lakes of the USSR
    VI: The Tundra
    VII: The Taiga
    VIII: In a Compound Forest
    IX: In the Blackland Steppes
    X: Along the Dry Steppes
    XI: In the Wastes
    XII: In the Caucasus
    XIII: In the Urals
    XIV: Moscow—Capital of the USSR
    XV: The Brotherly Union of the Soviet Peoples

## FIFTH GRADE

*Title: Physical Geography*

*Chapter*

    I: Diagrams and Maps
    II: Dry-land Surfaces

III: The Waters of the Earth
IV: Forms and Movements of the Earth
V: Weather and Climate
VI: Measuring Dry-land Surfaces
VII: The Zones of Nature
VIII: Population

# SIXTH GRADE

*Title: Parts of the World*

## I. EUROPE

General Physical-Geographical Survey
Land Surfaces
Climate
Internal Bodies of Water
Natural Zones
Population and Political Maps

## II. ASIA

General Physical-Geographical Survey
Land Surfaces
Climate
Inland Bodies of Water
Natural Zones
Population and Political Maps

## III. AFRICA

General Physical-Geographical Survey and Population
Natural Zones

## IV. AMERICA

General Physical-Geographical Survey
North America

Natural Zones
South America
Natural Zones
Population and Political Maps

### V. AUSTRALIA

General Physical-Geographical Survey and Population

### VI. ANTARCTICA

General Physical-Geographical Survey

## SEVENTH GRADE

*Title: Physical Geography of the USSR*

### I. GENERAL SURVEY OF THE USSR

Geographical Conditions and Borders
Seas of the USSR
Terrain of the USSR
Climate of the USSR
Internal Bodies of Water of the USSR
Natural Zones of the USSR
Population of the USSR
Political Maps of the USSR
National Economy of the USSR

### II. SURVEY OF THE USSR ACCORDING TO PHYSICAL-GEOGRAPHICAL REGIONS

Eastern European Plains Area
The Urals
Western Siberia
Eastern Siberia

The Far East
The Caucasus
Central Asia and Kazakstan


# EIGHTH GRADE

*Title: Economic Geography of Foreign Countries*

## EUROPE

The Polish People's Republic
The Czechoslovakian Republic
The Hungarian People's Republic
The Rumanian People's Republic
The Bulgarian People's Republic
The People's Republic of Albania
The Federated People's Republic of Yugoslavia
Germany
Great Britain
France
Belgium
Luxemburg
The Netherlands
Switzerland
Austria
Italy
Spain
Portugal
Greece
Finland
Sweden
Norway
Denmark
Iceland

### ASIA

The Chinese People's Republic
The Mongolian People's Republic
Korea
Vietnam
India
Nepal. Ceylon
Pakistan
The Countries of Southeast Asia
Burma
Thailand. Laos, Cambodia, Malaya
Indonesia
The Philippines
Japan
Afghanistan
Iran
Turkey
Countries of Southwest Asia

### AMERICA

The United States of America
Canada
Latin America

### AFRICA

### AUSTRALIA AND THE EAST INDIES

# NINTH GRADE

*Title: Economic Geography of the USSR*

## GENERAL SURVEY OF THE USSR AND ITS BASIC ECONOMIC BRANCHES

I: Characteristics of the National Economy of the USSR
II: Geography of Heavy Industry in the USSR
III: Geography of the Rural Economy of the USSR
IV: Geography of Light Industry in the USSR
V: Geography of Transportation of the USSR

## GENERAL SURVEY OF THE UNITED REPUBLICS AND REGIONS OF THE USSR

I: Russian Soviet Federation of the Socialistic Republics
II: The Ukrainian SSR
III: The Moldavian SSR
IV: The Byelorussian SSR
V: Union of Baltic Republics
VI: The United Republics of Transcaucasia
VII: Kazakstan SSR
VIII: United Republics of Central Asia
IX: Economic Unity of the USSR and a Perspective of the Development of Its National Economy

# 6

## CONCLUSIONS AND
## RECOMMENDATIONS

The foregoing chapters seem to establish that the curriculum and the textbooks of the Soviet school system provide Soviet students with a vastly greater knowledge of literature, foreign languages, history, and geography than the American school system provides our students.

These comparisons suggest that there are four basic reasons that Soviet students enjoy this enormous advantage. First, the Soviet curriculum requires that Soviet students spend many hours and many years studying all of these basic subjects. Second, the continuity of the subject matter at successive grade levels is so carefully preserved that Soviet students gain immensely from the orderliness, the systematic presentation, and the perspective which only such a continuity can provide. Third, Soviet students are taught to read so efficiently and effectively during the first four grades that in the fifth they are prepared to study literature, foreign languages, history, and geography on a surprisingly mature level; and fourth, Soviet textbooks are carefully written by competent scholars.

On the other hand, American students are deprived of a solid knowledge of literature, foreign languages, history, and geography because, first, they spend far fewer hours and years studying them; second, because the continuity of these basic subjects from grade to grade is commonly not only lacking, but oftentimes the study of the subject itself is interrupted for semesters or years at a time; third, the vocabulary in American basal readers is so small that unless students have learned to read from sources other than these readers, they have still not mastered reading skills by the sixth or even the eighth grade, and are therefore unable to cope with textbooks which have any degree of maturity at all; and fourth, American textbooks are commonly not only badly written but written to appeal to students of a relatively low degree of intelligence, and they are often written by authors who do not have nearly the competence required to write a good textbook.

These conclusions about the teaching of literature, history, foreign languages, and geography in American schools are not wild charges; they may be substantiated and documented endlessly by an examination of the curriculum and textbooks of almost all the public and parochial schools in the United States.

I should like to make clear, however, that I am not saying no American students between the first and the twelfth grades acquire a close knowledge of these subjects, because some obviously do. What I am saying is that if students have learned to read well in the elementary grades, they did not learn to do so from their basal readers; that if they have an adequate knowledge of American, English and world literature, they did not acquire it from typical American textbooks through the tenth grade; that if they have a solid knowledge of history and geography, they probably owe no great debt to the curriculum of their schools and probably even less to their textbooks; and that if they have a *good* knowledge of a foreign language they may be among the mere 2 or 3 per cent of high school graduates who are able to acquire such knowledge from our public and parochial schools.

It is perhaps impossible to say how many students are able

to acquire a respectable knowledge of these subjects with the help of their parents at home or their teachers through outside or special assignments, but the generally disappointing results of tests administered by the army would indicate that the number is very small indeed.

It would be a serious error, however, to suppose that only the Soviet schools demand that students acquire a sound knowledge of literature, foreign languages, history, and geography. Soviet education, in point of fact, is merely a part of the great tradition of European education, and has been since the time of Catherine II. With but a few exceptions, the curriculum of the Soviet schools and the curriculum of the schools in any Western European country are virtually indistinguishable.

What distinguishes the Soviet school system most sharply from the school systems of Western Europe is not the curriculum or the demands that are made upon the student, but the orientation of the schools to the promotion of the Communist cause. The overriding aim of Soviet education is to promote Communist doctrines and the Communist system generally; it is not calculated to develop the human person as a person without reference to his contribution to the advancement of communism.

The humanities—literature, history, philosophy, art, and theology—are traditionally the areas of human knowledge which most carefully preserve and propagate the values and ideas that mark men as truly and peculiarly human persons and which affirm far better than any other areas of knowledge the dignity of the human person. The humanities also reaffirm spiritual qualities of man which are inviolable and which in particular are not subject to the laws of the society in which he lives. It is this latter function of the humanities that has led many people, particularly Americans, to believe that the Soviet education system suppresses the humanities. It does indeed suppress the study of theology in order to establish a belligerent atheism, and it limits philosophical inquiry largely to the Marx-ist-Leninist framework. But as we have seen, the Soviet education system, far from suppressing literature and history, in fact emphasizes them and turns them to the advantage of communism.

Soviet students are provided with a thorough knowledge of the literature of their country so that they may understand that some of the greatest literary minds of the past have foreseen that the deprivations and subjugation of the working classes in the eighteenth and nineteenth centuries were due first to the evils of the feudal system and later of the capitalistic system, and that only with the growth of communism have the working classes been able to achieve dignity and live a decent life. By reading selected works from these pre-Soviet authors, Soviet students not only *see* the pre-Revolutionary miseries of the Russian people, but also, since imaginative literature appeals strongly to the emotions, *feel* them too, just as by reading Soviet literature they can both see and feel the glories of communism. Thus, a thorough knowledge of Russian literature can condition a student's will so that, emotionally as well as rationally, he becomes convinced of the superiority of the Communist system.

Similarly, Soviet students are given a thorough knowledge of the history of Western civilization because they can thus be made to believe that the slaveholding system of ancient civilizations, the feudal system of the Middle Ages, and the capitalistic system of the eighteenth and nineteenth centuries were merely imperfect governmental and economic systems which led to the establishment of a superior and terminal Communist system. This detailed and carefully presented view of history provides Soviet students with a historical perspective so clear and so persuasive that they feel a sense of the destiny of the triumph of communism, which is precisely the effect the Soviet education system intends to produce.

Soviet textbooks in literature and history are thus carefully designed to provide students with an abundance of literary experiences and historical proof which will persuade them of the superiority and destiny of communism. In the literature text-books this aim commonly results in a misrepresentation of the ideas and attitudes of famous Russian authors of the eighteenth and nineteenth centuries, not basically through any tampering with their works, but by a careful selection of them and, in the later grades, by a distortion of literary history. In history text-books this aim results in a serious distortion of the events of the past, again not so much by a deliberate altering of historical facts but by a careful selection of facts and a dishonest interpretation of them. Nonetheless, Soviet students, as we have seen, are given a thorough knowledge of the literature and history of their country, for the assumption is that the firmer the knowledge of these subjects, the firmer will be the student's conviction of the superiority and eventual world-wide triumph of communism.

Nor is it difficult to understand why the Soviet education system places great emphasis upon foreign languages. No country, perhaps, is more aware than the Soviet Union of the immense political and propaganda value of foreign languages. The educational authorities of Soviet schools are fully aware that among the best weapons to beat down anti-Communist opposition is a large number of its own people who can read the literature and write and speak the language of its adversaries or its potential allies. The Soviet government knows that these countries are not going to be persuaded of the advantages of communism if the arguments, printed or spoken, are presented in an unknown tongue. Ten million Russians are not learning English because they love America.

Likewise, the reason Soviet education attaches so much importance to geography is plain enough. In the first place, much of the effectiveness of a student's knowledge of history, economics, political science, and current events depends upon his knowledge of geography; secondly, it is good for all citizens of a Communist country to have a detailed knowledge of which territories communism has already conquered and which territories are yet to be conquered. The recent emphasis upon economic geography in the upper grades merely serves better than anything else to demonstrate to Soviet students the economic superiority of the Communist system.

It must not be thought that the major reorganization the Soviet schools are now undergoing will lead to a reduction in the amount of time devoted to the humanities. It is true that the law which was passed by the Supreme Soviet in December 1958 calls for a significant increase in the time students devote to polytechnical skills. Nonetheless, at the same time, the so-called "incomplete" high school program is to be expanded from seven grades to eight, and the "complete" high school program from ten grades to eleven, so that much of the increased emphasis upon polytechnical training poses no threat to the time devoted to the humanities. Furthermore, the law itself warns against any reduction in the humanities, and on this point reads as follows:

> The reorganization of the schools should by no means result in a reduction or weakening of education in the humanities, which is of great importance for the formation of the pupils' Communist world outlook.
>
> —*Strengthening the Ties of the School with Life, and Further Developing the System of Public Education.* Soviet Booklet No. 4. Soviet Booklets, London, December 1958, p. 12.

In fact, in the reorganized program for the new eight-year school, present provisions call for 1,662 school hours to be devoted to the humanities as opposed to 1,400 in the old seven-year school. (Elizabeth Moos, *Soviet Education Today and Tomorrow.* The National Council of American-Soviet Friendship, New York, p. 33.)

It is perhaps well to say once again that the point at issue is

not simply the difference between Soviet and American education but between American education and European education
in general. Whatever else is true of the European system of
education, it has rightly held that a sound knowledge of literature, history, foreign languages, the basic sciences (physics,
chemistry, biology), mathematics, and geography are so funda-
mental to the welfare of the individual as well as the nation
that students must study these subjects thoroughly and systematically over a period of many years. The European education system holds, furthermore, that the primary purpose of
the schools is to see that students acquire this knowledge.

The American school system, on the other hand, seems during the past thirty years to have come to believe that it is not
very important for our students to have a thorough knowledge
of these basic subjects, but that it is important that they be
thoroughly familiar with the minutiae of community living and
that they should above all learn to become adjusted to their
environment as they find it. As a result, a great deal of the time
our students spend in class in both the grade schools and the
high schools is taken up with learning things which have nothing, or virtually nothing, to do with the basic subjects.

It is commonly said in defense of the present practices of our
American schools that the job of the schools is to educate all
the students, not merely an intellectual elite. But in reply it
must be observed that it is precisely the aim of the Soviet seven-
year (and now eight-year) schools to educate all students too,
and yet it is primarily in the first seven or eight years that the
curriculum and textbooks of American schools compare so badly
with those of Soviet schools. It is also commonly said in defense
of our schools that our education system is "best for our society." The implication is that in a highly democratic society
such as ours, learning the basic subjects well is not really very
important. But this position is patently false, and it is in the
prevalence of this attitude that much of the danger to our
educational system lies.

American schools have not, of course, abandoned the basic subjects entirely: all our students do study their own language, though they don't learn it very well; they all do study literature, though not very much or very good literature; they all do study history and geography, though not very much for very long; they all do study mathematics, though many never get beyond arithmetic; most of them study a basic science, though for only a year; and some of them study a foreign language, but not long enough to learn it. Clearly, then, American schools, merely by virtue of the fact that the curriculum provides for the study of at least most of the basic subjects, have not abandoned the belief in the importance of these subjects, but as the foregoing chapters have shown, they have tragically abandoned thorough instruction in them. And herein lies the crucial difference not merely between American education and Soviet education, but between American education and European education.

Whatever may be said in criticism of European education, it must be said that no European nation permits its students to go to school for six years without learning to read more than 4,000 different words from their readers. No European nation lets its students go to school for ten years without giving them a close acquaintance with the major literary works in their language; no European nation lets its students graduate from high school without a relatively sound knowledge of the history and geography of their country and of the world which enables them to orient themselves in time and in space. No European nation permits its students to go to school for eight or twelve years without learning to read and write at least one foreign language. No European nation lets its school children reach the age of fourteen without a knowledge of mathematics that does not exceed simple arithmetic; and no European nation lets its students go to school for nine years without studying physics or chemistry or biology.

It is not intellectual backwardness that explains the tremendous emphasis of the Soviet and European education systems upon these basic subjects, and it is not intellectual enlightenment and progress that explain why American education neglects them. The basis and structure of knowledge is the same on one side of the Atlantic Ocean as it is on the other; it does not change its character in transit. The wisdom of Europe and of the ages has recognized the supreme importance of the study of language, literature, history, geography, mathematics, and the basic sciences in the intellectual development of all men, and that without such knowledge, men are intellectually paralyzed.

If, in the years to come, the world should be fortunate enough to escape a third world war, then the world will enter into a state of competitive co-existence between the free world and communism. The role of the American school system in this competition must be to strengthen the intellectual resources of America by making certain that our children receive a solid knowledge of the basic subjects in our schools.

This means that American schools must without delay make major and, where necessary, drastic reforms to insure that our students acquire a solid knowledge not only of mathematics and the basic sciences, but also of their own language and the languages of other countries, of the literature of their own country and of other countries as well, of the history and geography of their own country and of the world. And, perhaps most important of all, our students must be taught to read early enough and well enough so that they will be equipped to begin the study of these subjects early and thoroughly.

I hope that I will be spared the charge that I am advocating that American schools imitate Soviet schools. Nothing perhaps impresses upon one the weaknesses of Soviet education so much as a reading of the textbooks used in Soviet schools. The knowledge which these textbooks provide is never knowledge for its own sake or knowledge intended to be used freely for whatever purposes students may later on desire to use it. It is always knowledge intended to strengthen and promote the cause of communism. Free inquiry into ideological areas is stifled as a matter of course. The treatment of American history in eighth- and ninth-grade history textbooks used in Soviet schools is in itself enough to condemn Soviet education as a process that brutally and viciously warps young minds. And the practice of requiring Soviet students to memorize and recite party-line opinions which are italicized in their textbooks is unspeakable. These and similar aspects of Soviet education are not only deplorable but horrifying.

By the same token, I should like to indicate that I recognize fully the many virtues of the American school system. No one who studies the history of our school system can fail to be impressed by its immense contribution to the growth and development of America as a strong democratic society. It has in the past also served admirably in the formation of intelligent and worthy American citizens and intelligent and worthy human beings; and the fact that it provides for the education of all Americans brings it the admiration of all the world.

However, as this and numerous other recent studies have shown, there has been a serious deterioration in the past thirty years in the intellectual content of the curriculum and textbooks of our public and parochial schools. In fact, the intellectual content of the American curriculum and textbooks is weakest at the very point in history when the times demand that it be strongest. Never before in the history of America has a rigorous intellectual program in our schools been more urgently needed. Without exaggerating, one may say that the continued existence of a free world may in large measure depend upon the establishment of such a program.

But in order that our public and parochial schools may adequately fulfill the needs of the nation and the needs of the students themselves, the schools must be willing to make major changes in the curriculum and textbooks for the purpose of strengthening instruction not merely in mathematics and the sciences, but also in the subjects which are concerned with ideas, i.e., the humanities and the subjects closely related to the humanities. It is quite as important that the ideological position of the free world be strengthened as it is that its technological position be strengthened, and it is through a renewed emphasis upon the humanities in our schools that our ideological position will be made more effective. To underestimate the importance of ideas in determining the course of history or in determining the course of the current struggle against communism itself is not to understand history.

Thus, if Soviet education can use literature as a highly effective means of persuading Soviet students of the superiority of the Communist way of life, then surely American education can give our students a thorough enough understanding of literature to reaffirm not only the dignity of man but the spiritual worth of the individual, and therefore to strengthen their faith and devotion to the democratic way of life which preserves that dignity and that spiritual worth. And if Soviet education can use history to persuade Soviet students that all political and economic systems are inferior to communism, then surely American education can teach our children enough of the history of the world to convince them honestly of the meaning and value of freedom in a democratic society. There is hardly a more effective way of giving students an understanding and appreciation of the democratic way of life in general and of America in particular than to provide them with a close knowledge of the civilizations and tyrannies of the past—and only a genuine and thorough study of history can provide that knowledge. It is primarily by means of the humanities, including literature and history, that we can most effectively not only puncture the Communist dialectic, but also strengthen our own faith in the importance of the spiritual worth of the individual and of human freedom.

Likewise, our schools will not be communistic if they adopt textbooks which can teach our children to read well by the end of the fourth grade, with a vocabulary of 7,000 or 8,000 words rather than the 1,500 words or less that are all that even the bright students now get from their readers; nor is it being communistic to require students to spend six or eight years learning to read, write, and speak a foreign language rather than the two years they now spend if they are among the 25 per cent who study one at all; and it is certainly not being communistic to give our students a thorough knowledge of the geography of the world and of America, so that history and economics and political science and current events can have some meaning for them.

Above all, it is not communistic for students to study hard in school and at home so that they can train their minds well enough to become the competent professional leaders and intelligent citizens that America and the free world desperately require. There is an inordinate fear among parents and even among school administrators and teachers that our children will be overworked in school and that they must have plenty of time for recreation. But as things stand now, they have nothing to fear. No children in the world are less overworked or more overrecreated than American children. They enjoy the freedom of long vacations; the vast majority of them enjoy a freedom from homework in the early grades and some even in the later grades, and many also enjoy a freedom from learning even during school hours. This fear that children will work too hard at their studies is merely one more manifestation of the anti-intellectual spirit that pervades so much of our thinking in this country. At the present time it is the least enlightened position that one can take, for unless we rise to the recognition that education is the bulwark of the free world, this unwillingness to permit children to work hard in school can do as much to bring about the destruction of the free world as any weapon in the Communist arsenal. We need to be reminded of Aristotle's maxim that all learning is accompanied by pain, and particularly the corollary that where there is no pain there is no learning. But it is just as true that learning can also be accompanied by pleasure, and most students derive much pleasure from being intellectually challenged.

There has, of course, been a growing realization in the past few years that all is not well in American education, and there have been some honest efforts to improve it. It should be pointed out, however, that such reforms as are now being carried on have largely been confined to the high schools. Except for a few efforts to teach foreign languages without textbooks and some isolated attempts to beef up mathematics, the elementary and junior high schools placidly maintain the status quo with apparent impunity. Yet, the record of our elementary and our junior high schools is far worse than even that of most of our high schools.

## SOME RECOMMENDATIONS

What, specifically, can the schools do in order to assure that our children acquire the thorough knowledge of the basic subjects which they must have in order to be reasonably well-educated men and women as well as good and useful citizens? The notion is common that the quality of American education cannot be improved without spending money; and many parents, teachers, and school administrators in communities where increased funds for schools are not available experience a sense of frustration and feel that their hands are tied.

But there is, in fact, a great deal that they can do to improve the quality of education in their schools, a great deal which does not cost money. It is quite true that solving the problems of the teacher shortage and the classroom shortage requires money, and a good deal of it. But the fact is that even if teachers were plentiful and well trained, even if classrooms were abundant and roomy and well lighted, and even if school buildings and school equipment were all new and shiny, students would still be likely to receive a poor education in the basic subjects if the curriculum and the textbooks remained poor.

And yet, it is a very consoling truth that a good textbook does not cost any more than a bad textbook, and it is just as true that a good curriculum does not cost any more money than a bad curriculum. In fact, a curriculum in which the humanities and the subjects directly related to the humanities are properly represented may well cost less than one in which they are not, because rarely is special and expensive equipment required in teaching these basic subjects.

Below are some rather specific suggestions as to what changes in textbooks and in the curriculum will greatly increase the effectiveness in teaching reading, literature, foreign languages, history, and geography in American grade schools and high schools, whether they are public or parochial.

## READING

Since reading is the key to a thorough knowledge of all the basic subjects, the most pressing need in the early grades is to develop a vastly more effective reading program than almost all the public and parochial schools in this country now have. In order to insure that the average student learns to read at a rate somewhat near that of which he is capable, he must be taught from readers that have three to five times the vocabulary and at least twice as much text as the typical reader series now has. A sixth-grade reader must have an absolute minimum of a 10,000-word vocabulary if it is to be at all adequate; good fourth-grade readers should have no less than a 5,000-word vocabulary, rather than the 1,200- or 1,500-word vocabulary that they now have; and second-grade readers must have a 2,000-word vocabulary rather than a 700-word vocabulary. I am not speaking here of supplementary readers, but of *basic* or basal readers from which *all* students learn to read, for even after due consideration has been given to "individual differences" there are very few students who are not capable of learning to read at the rate I have indicated, and many can learn at a much faster rate.

To teach students to read at this rate is neither impossible nor even difficult. Nor is this recommendation radical: Soviet students, as we have seen, are taught to read at an even faster rate, and European students generally, including British students, learn at as fast a rate. The McGuffey readers of the last century assumed that students read at least as quickly as I have suggested, and the fifth- and sixth-grade McGuffey readers assumed that they can learn to read much faster.

School administrators and teachers may argue among themselves as to the best means to teach reading from second-grade readers with a 2,000-word vocabulary and sixth-grade readers with a 10,000- to 15,000-word vocabulary. *The only intolerable argument is that it cannot be done.*

But regardless of what methods are decided upon to teach students to read at the rate at which they should learn to read, the main point is that the typical reader series now used in the schools is wholly inadequate. Parents themselves can usually recognize whether the readers from which their children are learning to read are inadequate by a quick examination of them. The readers of most of these series, particularly for the first four grades, have some sort of "vocabulary information" in the back pages which indicates how large or how small the vocabulary in the book is and how the words are handled. If this information corresponds at all to that described in the first chapter of this book, or if the reader belongs to any of the reader series listed on pages 17-18 of this book, parents can be certain that the reading program in their children's school is very poor. In fact, in the face of the evidence, no school authority who undertakes to defend the typical reader series as described in Chapter 1 of this book or as listed on pages 17-18 can any longer be said to have the interests of American education at heart.

The most urgent step, then, to be taken in order to insure a satisfactory reading program in American elementary schools might be outlined as follows:

*Adopt basic readers which have a vocabulary of not less than 10,000 words at the sixth-grade level, not less than 5,000 words at the fourth-grade level, and not less than 2,000 words at the second-grade level.*

It will be seen that elementary readers which have as large a vocabulary as they ought to have can also contain selections which are not only interesting and exciting, but which are also highly rewarding—as the selections in the typical reader series now in use commonly are not. Thus, just as proper methods and proper readers can teach children to read well, so proper selections can teach them to enjoy reading.

The establishing of a good reading program in the elementary grades is so vital that unless it is done, attempts to improve the teaching of all the other basic subjects will flounder.

## LITERATURE

One of the cardinal functions of American schools is to see that American students get a good literary education. Unfortunately, however, students can acquire a good literary education only by reading and studying literature over a period of many years. The student's literary education ought ideally to begin in the first grade and continue through the twelfth. Actually, there is no reason why it cannot, since "English," or "language arts" as it is now more commonly called, is taught at every grade level. In fact, the primary problem of giving our students a good literary education is not one of curriculum, but of textbooks.

The first and second chapters of this book have shown that even the best of the typical reader series now used in our elementary schools make a negligible contribution to our children's literary education. Therefore, any elementary school system that uses them is bound to have an ineffective literature program, because no elementary school can rely exclusively upon a "supplementary" or upon a "voluntary" reading program. Too many students can successfully escape such a program, and many of the supplementary readers and books are no more literary than the typical basal readers.

Therefore, to insure that the maximum number of children receive the best literary education possible in the early grades, elementary schools must depend chiefly on basic readers that contain the best possible selections rather than the worst possible selections. In addition, every encouragement should, of course, be given to as many children as possible to read good books in or out of the classroom.

If second graders are taught to read from readers with a 2,000-word vocabulary, then these readers can draw from an unbelievably rich store of fables, fairy tales, folk tales, and children's poems and stories which are a part of the literary heritage not merely of America but of the world. Not only should our children read these stories and poems, but they will take immense delight in reading them.

In order that the reader may see how literary an American sixth-grade reader can be, and in fact has been, below is reprinted from the Table of Contents of a sixth-grade McGuffey Reader the authors there represented. (The figures in parentheses indicate the number of selections by each author if there is more than one selection):

| | |
|---|---|
| Addison, Joseph (2) | Atherstone, Edwin |
| Arnold, George | Bacon, Sir Francis |

Beecher, Lyman (2)
Bible, The (3)
Blackstone, Sir William
Blackwood's Magazine
Brown, John
Browning, Elizabeth B.
Bryant, William Cullen (3)
Bulwer-Lytton, Sir Edward
  George
Burke, Edmund
Byrd, William
Byron, George Gordon
  (Lord) (3)
Calhoun, John C.
Campbell, Thomas (2)
Cary, Alice
Channing, William Ellery
Chorley, H. F.
Coleridge, Samuel Taylor
Colman, George
Cowper, William
Dana, Richard H., Jr.
Davy, Sir Humphry
Dewey, Orville
Dickens, Charles
Disraeli, Benjamin
Drake, Joseph Rodman
Dryden, John
Dwight, Timothy
Emerson, Ralph Waldo
Everett, Edward
Fields, James T.
Flagg, Wilson
Fox, Charles James
Franklin, Benjamin
Goldsmith, Oliver
Gratian, Henry
Gray, Thomas

Greeley, Horace
Greenwood, F. W. P.
Grimke, Thomas
Halleck, Fitz-Greene
Hayne, Robert Young
Hazlitt, William
Hemans, Felicia D.
Henry, Patrick
Holmes, Oliver Wendell (2)
Hood, Thomas
Hopkinson, Francis
Howells, William Dean
Howitt, William
Hunt, Leigh
Hutton, Joseph
Irving, Washington (3)
Jackson, Helen Hunt
Jefferson, Thomas
Johnson, Samuel (2)
Jones, Sir William
Kennedy, John P.
King, Thomas Starr
Lee, Henry
Lefebvre-Laboulaye, Edouard
Longfellow, Henry Wadsworth (4)
Macaulay, Thomas Babington
Mackenzie, Henry
Milton, John
Mitford, Mary Russell
Neal, John
Parkman, Francis
Percival, J. G.
Phillips, Charles
Pierpont, John
Pitt, Sir William
Poe, Edgar Allan
Pope, Alexander
Porter, Noah

Prentice, George D.
Prescott, William
Procter, Adelaide Anne
Read, T. B.
Rogers, Samuel
Ruskin, John
Scott, Sir Walter (4)
Shakespeare, William (9)
Sheridan, Richard Brinsley
Simms, William Gilmore
Sparks, Jared
Sprague, Charles
Spring, Gardiner
Sumner, Charles
Taylor, Bayard
Tennyson, Alfred Lord
Thackeray, William Makepeace

Thomson, James
Thrale, Hester Lynch
Timrod, Henry
Tobin, John
Tyndall, John
Von Herder, J. G.
Waller, Edmund
Walpole, Sir Robert
Webster, Daniel (3)
Whitney, Adeline
Whittier, John Greenleaf (2)
Wilson, John C.
Winthrop, R. C.
Wirt, William
Wordsworth, Samuel
Wordsworth, William

The reader may ascertain how far the literary quality of modern readers and anthologies has deteriorated by comparing these authors with the ones represented in any typical reader now used in the sixth, seventh, eighth, ninth, and even the tenth grade. (See the tables of contents reprinted at the end of Chapter 2.)

But in order that sixth graders may be prepared to read selections by authors comparable to many of those listed above, they must, of course, be given the opportunity in the earlier grades to read literary selections that are challenging enough to correspond with their capabilities. And this practice should reach all the way back to the first grade.

Beginning in the seventh grade, literature should be studied systematically and from genuine literary anthologies which introduce students to the best authors, rather than from mere readers which introduce them to the fourth- and fifth-rate authors.

The seventh- and eighth-grade literature courses might be

organized around literary genres or authors, so that by the ninth grade it might be appropriate to introduce the chronological study of literature.

It is clear, however, that in order to institute immediately an effective literature program in the junior high schools, much care must be taken to choose the best textbooks, since most of those now on the market are totally unsatisfactory. The use of paperback books at the junior high level should be considered strongly wherever first-rate literature anthologies are not available, or until they are made available.

In the senior high schools, the tenth- and eleventh-grade literature courses should give students an even closer acquaintance not only with American literature but with English literature—and with the historical development of literature. The twelfth-grade literature course might well be given over to a study of world literature, so that students can become acquainted with some of the major literary works of other countries and other cultures, including a selection of Greek and Latin classics. There would appear to be no defense for the practice in almost half the high schools in this country of not requiring English in the twelfth grade.

These recommendations for improving the literature program in American schools may, then, be summarized as follows:

### At the Elementary School Level

Use *basic* readers with selections which acquaint students in all the elementary grades with the rich literary heritage which the English language offers, as virtually none of the basal reader series now do.

### At the Junior High School Level

Use literature textbooks or paperback books which introduce students to the lives and works of the best English and

American authors, not merely the third and fourth best. These textbooks should also introduce students to a systematic study of literary theory, literary types, literary movements and, to some extent, literary chronology and history.

### At the Senior High School Level

1. Require English in the twelfth grade wherever it is not already required.
2. Wherever possible, relegate the "types" course to the junior high grades, to insure that every student takes at least one year of American literature and one year of English literature.
3. Offer a course in world literature in the twelfth grade.

Most of the recommendations made here to improve the literature program in the schools do not require any basic changes in the curriculum. The problem is simply one of assuring more students of getting a far better literary education than most of them now get, and it is a problem that in the long run requires little or no money to solve.

## FOREIGN LANGUAGES

It will be readily evident that the chief difficulty with the foreign-language program of most American schools is a problem of curriculum. The greatest need is to increase the foreign-language requirement at the high school level from two to four years. As I have already indicated, this increase could be brought about most effectively—and, in fact, most properly—if colleges and universities were to include four years of a foreign language among their admissions requirements; but until such a requirement is forthcoming, the high schools will have to take the initiative themselves if students are to acquire a truly effective knowledge of a foreign language. Urging more students to study a foreign language and introducing foreign languages into high schools which do not now offer them are also highly important measures.

The elementary schools need and deserve every possible encouragement to introduce foreign languages into the early grades. However, before basing language teaching at this level solely on the conversational approach, there should be real proof that the approach works, that students are actually learning to speak the language and are not merely picking up a few phrases here and there and forgetting even these over the summer vacation. School authorities would do very well indeed to also consider teaching foreign languages with the use of textbooks, since there is no doubt that children can learn to read a foreign language in the classroom, even though they may not be able to make much headway in learning to speak it.

In any case, time devoted to studying foreign languages in the elementary schools will largely turn out to be time wasted unless there are provisions to continue the study of the language in the junior high school grades. Thus, a massive coordinating effort will be required if such a program is to be made effective.

It must be realized above all, however, that any foreign-language program is a failure if it does not give students a *good* reading knowledge or a *good* speaking knowledge of the language.

Recommendations for assuring successful foreign-language programs in our schools may be summarized, then, as follows:

### At the Elementary and Junior High Level

1. Introduce the teaching of foreign languages in the elementary grades, provided there is some chance that the program will succeed and provided that it can eventually be correlated with neighboring junior high school programs.

2. Consider the manifest advantages of basing a foreign-language program in the elementary and junior high grades upon the use of textbooks rather than exclusively upon a conversational approach.

### At the High School Level

1. Require four years of a foreign language, beginning with the ninth grade.
2. Urge or require many more students to study a foreign language.

## HISTORY

The effective teaching of history is, like the teaching of foreign languages, also primarily a matter of improving the curriculum. American history, instead of being taught for three years at three-year intervals, is much better taught at the junior high level, ending with the ninth or tenth grade and presented in a three-year sequence of courses in order that students may study it in the detail that they should. Similarly, if the world-history program is to be at all adequate it must be represented by at least a two-year sequence of courses rather than by the one-year tenth-grade course that now prevails. Like the American-history sequence, the world-history sequence should also be required, not merely elective.

The elementary schools can best do their part by making provisions for a year-long introductory course in American history and another year-long introductory course in world history, regardless of whatever other social studies activities are carried on.

Thus, the most important recommendations for improving the history programs in American schools would include the following:

### At the Elementary School Level

1. Establish a one-year introductory course in American history.
2. Establish a one-year introductory course in world history or world civilizations.

### At the High School Level

1. Establish a three-year sequence of American-history courses required of all students somewhere between the seventh and twelfth grades.
2. Establish a two-year sequence of world-history courses required of all students somewhere between the ninth and twelfth grades.

## GEOGRAPHY

The geography curriculum must also be greatly strengthened if American students are to acquire anything like an adequate knowledge of geography. In the elementary grades neither history nor geography is likely to be taught effectively unless they are taught during the same term rather than in alternate semesters. And to combine them, as some textbooks do, is, as we have seen, merely to weaken the teaching of both.

A good geography program can, and probably should, terminate at the end of the ninth grade, but if the program is to be effective, students will need to spend approximately twice as much time studying geography as they now do, and they must study it from efficient and worth-while geography textbooks.

The minimum geography program which would cover all the basic aspects of geography would be as follows:

1. Establish a full two-year introductory course in geography at the elementary level.

2. Establish a full two-year course in physical and economic geography at the junior high school level.
3. Select geography textbooks which present the subject thoroughly and systematically and yet interestingly and which therefore avoid the fragmentary and watered-down presentation of many geographies now in use.

The foregoing suggestions are offered merely as guides. The danger of making recommendations of this sort too specific are almost as great as not making them specific enough. But it is hoped that those offered here will at least give some indication as to what might—indeed, what *must*—be done to improve instruction in these basic subjects. A few schools have already made major changes in order to strengthen the teaching of the basic subjects, and many have at least made a beginning, but many others, particularly at the elementary and junior high school levels, have not even done that.

It will be observed that in order to improve the foreign-language and history and geography programs, these recommendations call for major revisions of the curriculum. And indeed major changes must be made if these basic subjects are to be taught at all adequately. In most schools this will involve not simply patchwork but a complete reorganization of the curriculum; some subjects will have to be entirely eliminated from the curriculum in order to give proper priority to the basic subjects. Great danger lies in devoting too many classroom hours to unessential subjects at the expense of the basic subjects, and yet no schools in the past thirty years have gone farther in giving priority to largely extraneous subjects than American schools.

But the times now require that parents and teachers and school administrators and members of school boards regard closely all the consequences of not giving American students a thorough education in the basic subjects. In reshaping the curriculum in our schools, administrators will henceforth have to make sharp and often painful distinctions between the courses that are absolutely necessary and those that are merely desirable.

But even after a curriculum has been established in which foreign languages and history and geography are properly emphasized, school authorities must also assure that these subjects are taught in thorough and systematic fashion. This they can best do by making certain that only the best possible textbooks are selected.

In many instances the efforts to improve the quality of education in our schools by reforming the curriculum and by adopting better textbooks will not be easy. Attempts to find really good textbooks will often be frustrated because it will seem that no such textbooks are on the market; and, indeed, in many instances they are not. Similarly, the machinery involved in changing the curriculum at any grade level is often extremely complicated, and the opposition to changing it can be fierce. Yet none of these obstacles are insurmountable. A serious demand for better textbooks on the part of school administrators, teachers, and parents will result in better textbooks being published.

One of the reasons that it is so difficult to find good textbooks is that too many influential educators are committed to highly dubious theories of education, which reduce the level of instruction to the lower third of the class, and which lead to the publication of textbooks that are in accord with these theories. Bad textbooks are copied by other bad textbooks and good textbooks are thus often driven out altogether. It is for this reason, for example, that the basal reader series listed on pages 17-18 are uniformly bad. This also explains why a large number of geographies and junior high school readers are also bad.

Those who are in charge of establishing educational standards in any school system are the ones in the best position to influence the choice of textbooks. It is their job not only to select the best possible texts available but also to demand that publishers publish good textbooks if good textbooks are not available. If they do not do both, then teachers and parents and those who are in a position of authority can play their part. An effortless inquiry will discover who is responsible for choosing the textbooks used in any school system, whether it is a teacher or a principal or a superintendent, or a committee, or whether the selection of the textbooks is made at a local level or by the state board of education or some other state organization. Thus, much can be done to see that the best available texts are used and that demands are made upon publishers to publish better textbooks by thoroughly competent authors. The fact that in many systems textbooks, once chosen, are used for a three- or four-year period suggests how grave a responsibility textbook-selectors have.

Wherever the responsibility can be pinpointed, the possibilities for improvement are strong. The chart which is given in Appendix D on page 212 of this book helps to fix the responsibility for the textbooks in all states, and is particularly helpful in providing information as to whether the choice of textbooks in any state is under state control.

The business of making certain that high-quality textbooks and a strong academic curriculum are introduced into the schools should have a particular meaning for parents who hope that their children will one day attend a college or university. Admissions officers are already looking unfavorably upon high school graduates who are ill prepared in reading, writing, history, geography, literature, and foreign languages, to say nothing of mathematics and the sciences. And in the coming years, as everyone knows, the scramble to get into a respectable college will become even more fierce.

The colleges and universities know that these are the subjects and skills which must be mastered before a student may be said to be educated and before he can acquire any degree of professional competence. The likelihood of high school graduates' being accepted by a good college or university and the likelihood of their being able to continue once they have been accepted are directly proportionate to how well they have learned the basic subjects in their elementary and high school years. No critics of our elementary schools and our high schools are more severe than college freshmen.

But whether the motives for improving the teaching of reading, literature, foreign languages, history, and geography in our schools reflect self-interest, or whether they stem from more patriotic or more philosophical and far-sighted considerations, the arguments for a drastic improvement in the textbooks and the curriculum in these subjects are overwhelming, and the arguments against a drastic improvement of them are indefensible.

# Appendixes

# APPENDIX A

# Curriculum for Schools of General Education R.S.F.S.R. in the Ten-Year School

| Subjects | Number of hours a week in each grade | | | | | | | | | | Total hours | |
|---|---|---|---|---|---|---|---|---|---|---|---|---|
| | 1 | 2 | 3 | 4 | 5 | 6 | 7 | 8 | 9 | 10 | By the week | By the year |
| 1 | 2 | 3 | 4 | 5 | 6 | 7 | 8 | 9 | 10 | 11 | 12 | 13 |
| 1. Russian language and literature | 13 | 13 | 13 | 9 | 9 | 8 | 6 | 6/5 | 4 | 4 | 84.5 | 2,788 |
| 2. Mathematics | 6 | 6 | 6 | 6 | 6 | 6 | 6 | 6 | 6 | 6 | 60 | 1,980 |
| 3. History | | | | 2 | 2 | 2 | 2 | 4 | 4 | 4 | 20 | 660 |
| 4. Constitution of the U.S.S.R. | | | | | | | 1 | | | | 1 | 33 |
| 5. Geography | | | | 2 | 3 | 2 | 2 | 2/3 | 3 | ---- | 14.5 | 479 |
| 6. Biology | | | | 2 | 2 | 2 | 2 | 2 | 1 | 1 | 12 | 396 |
| 7. Physics | | | | | | 2 | 3 | 3 | 4 | 5/4 | 16.5 | 544 |
| 8. Astronomy | | | | | | | | | | 1 | 1 | 33 |
| 9. Chemistry | | | | | | | 2 | 2 | 3 | 3/4 | 10.5 | 347 |
| 10. Psychology | | | | | | | | | | 1 | 1 | 33 |
| 11. Foreign language | | | | | 4 | 4 | 3 | 3 | 3 | 3 | 20 | 660 |
| 12. Physical education | 2 | 2 | 2 | 2 | 2 | 2 | 2 | 2 | 2 | 2 | 20 | 660 |
| 13. Drawing | 1 | 1 | 1 | 1 | 1 | 1 | | | | | 6 | 198 |
| 14. Technical drawing | | | | | | | 1 | 1 | 1 | 1 | 4 | 132 |
| 15. Singing | 1 | 1 | 1 | 1 | 1 | 1 | | | | | 6 | 198 |
| 16. Work and practical exercises | 1 | 1 | 1 | 1 | 2 | 2 | 2 | | | | 10 | 330 |
| 17. Practice in agriculture with agricultural machinery and in electrotechnology | | | | | | | | 2 | 2 | 2 | 6 | 198 |
| 18. Excursions | | | | | | | | | | | | 188 |
| Total | 24 | 24 | 24 | 26 | 32 | 32 | 32 | 33 | 33 | 33 | 293 | 9,857 |

Figures divided by a diagonal line indicate number of hours per semester.

Source: E. N. Medynskii, *Prosveshchenie v. SSSR* (Education in the U.S.S.R.), Moscow, 1955, p. 84.

# APPENDIX B

# Some Basic Facts About Russian Schools

Soviet students enter the first grade at age 7.

They attend school six days a week.

The school term begins September 1 and continues for 34-35 weeks with two twelve-day vacations, one in January and one in March.

The curriculum described on the preceding page is a general curriculum, and is virtually the same for all students. There is no college preparatory curriculum as such. The percentage of students who fail to complete the first seven years is very small. In the urban areas, between 70 and 80 per cent go on to complete the last three years of the general curriculum described on the preceding page. About half of the students in the rural areas complete the ten-year school. Approximately 30 per cent of those graduating from the ten-year school go on to higher education, though large numbers of these are enrolled in evening or correspondence courses.

The plan for reorganizing the school as adopted by the Supreme Soviet in December 1958 extends the seven-year school to eight and the ten-year school to eleven years, so that hereafter all students will be required to attend school for eight years. This law became effective in September 1959, but the reorganization is not expected to be complete until 1964. Essentially the law calls for increased emphasis upon polytechnical skills, but the amount of time devoted to the basic academic subjects is not vitally affected, and in some instances it is increased, so that even now the curriculum here described has been but little altered.

# A Typical American Elementary School Curriculum

Elementary school curricula vary widely from state to state and from locality to locality. The following chart therefore describes the curriculum only in its broad outlines.

| Subject | Grade I | Grade II | Grade III | Grade IV | Grade V | Grade VI |
|---|---|---|---|---|---|---|
| LANGUAGE ARTS | Reading Language Hand-writing | Reading Language Spelling Hand-writing | Reading Language Spelling Hand-writing | Reading Language Spelling Hand-writing | Reading Language Spelling Hand-writing | Reading Language Spelling Hand-writing |
| MATHEMATICS | Arith-metic | Arith-metic | Arith-metic | Arith-metic | Arith-metic | Arith-metic |
| SOCIAL STUDIES | Urban and Rural Life | Urban and Rural Life | Urban and Rural Life | History and Ge-ography | History and Ge-ography | History and Ge-ography |
| ART, MUSIC, HEALTH, SAFETY, RECREATION | Art Music Health Safety Recrea-tion | Art Music Health Safety Recrea-tion | Art Music Health Safety Recrea-tion | Art Music Health Safety Recrea-tion | Art Music Health Safety Recrea-tion | Art Music Health Safety Recrea-tion |
| SCIENCE | General Science | General Science | General Science | General Science | General Science | General Science |

# APPENDIX C

# An American High School Curriculum, College Preparatory

High school curricula vary widely throughout the United States. A non-college preparatory curriculum may look very much different from this one, and this one is itself more nearly an optimum college preparatory curriculum than a typical one. Classroom time for each subject is considered to be five hours weekly otherwise indicated.

| Subject | Grade VII | Grade VIII | Grade IX | Grade X | Grade XI | Grade XII |
|---|---|---|---|---|---|---|
| LANGUAGE ARTS | Literature Language | Literature Language | Literature Language | Literature Language | American Literature | English Literature |
| SOCIAL STUDIES | Geography | American History | Civics | World History | American History | Contemporary Problems |
| MATHEMATICS | General | General | Algebra | Geometry | Algebra | Solid Geometry Trigonometry |
| SCIENCE | General | General | General | Biology | Physics | Chemistry |
| FOREIGN LANGUAGE | | | Two years of a foreign language between the 9th and 12th grades: Latin, Spanish, French, or German | | | |
| PHYSICAL EDUCATION | 2-3 hours | 2-3 hours | 2-3 hours | 2-3 hours | 2-3 hours | 2-3 hours |
| ELECTIVES* | 5-10 hours | 5-10 hours | 5-10 hours | 5-10 hours | 5-10 hours | 5-10 hours |

* Possible electives in many high schools are numerous, and at various grade levels may include among others the following: art, music, homemaking, shop, speech, typing, commercial courses, geography, world literature, problems in democracy, modern history, psychology, sociology, and driver training.

# APPENDIX D

## State Textbook Selection, as of December 1955

Column legend (numbered as in the table):

1. State
2. Each local school authority adopts own textbooks without recommendation or control from any State authority
3. Local school authority selects for each subject from a list of books approved by higher authority — Name of higher authority
4. One textbook for each subject
5. Multiple textbooks for each subject
6. Multiple textbooks for some subjects
7. State department of education adopts textbooks for all schools — One textbook for each subject
8. Multiple textbooks for each subject
9. Multiple textbooks for some subjects
10. State adoptions made by textbook commission under other authority than State department of education — Name of higher authority
11. Nature of board membership
12. Qualifications required of commission members
13. One textbook for each subject
14. Multiple textbooks for each subject
15. Multiple textbooks for some subjects
16. Factors in decisions — Years an adoption made by a State dept. or other State board holds
17. Authority that decides length of period which adoption holds
18. (Factors in decisions)
19. Number of State textbook libraries or laboratories maintained in State where textbooks may be studied by teachers and administrators

| 1 | 2 | 3 | 4 | 5 | 6 | 7 | 8 | 9 | 10 | 11 | 12 | 13 | 14 | 15 | 16 | 17 | 18 | 19 |
|---|---|---|---|---|---|---|---|---|----|----|----|----|----|----|----|----|----|----|
| Alabama | X | State board of education. | X | | X | | | | | | | | | | 4 | State textbook committee. | | 112 |
| Arizona | | State board of education. | | | | X | | | | | | | | | 5 | Legislature. | Finances, time subject areas. | 3 |
| Arkansas | | State board of education. | | X | | | X | | | | | | | | 4–6 | State board of education. | Act 103, General Assembly. | 1 |
| California | | State board of education. | | | | | | | | | | | | | 6–8 | do. | Time. | |
| Colorado | X | | | | | | | | | | | | | | | | | 4 |
| Connecticut | X | | | | | | X | | | | | | | | | | | 31 |
| Delaware | | State board of education. | | X | | | | | | | | | | | 4 | State board of education. | Staff recommendation. | 1 |
| Florida | | State board of education. | | X | | | | | State law | X | X | | | X | 3 | do. | Recommendation of textbook committee. | 71 |
| Georgia | | State board of education. | | X | | | | | | | | | | | 5 | do. | | |
| Idaho | | State curriculum development and textbook committee. | | X | | | X | | State board of education. | X | X | | X | | 5 | do. | | 5 |
| Illinois | X | | | | | | | | | | | | | | | | | 1 |
| Indiana | X | Commission on textbook adoption of the Indiana State Board of education. | X | | | | X | | | | | | | | 5 | General assembly. | Time. | 4 |
| Iowa | X | | | | | | | | | | | | | | | | | |
| Kansas | | State textbook commission. | X | | | | | | State Board of education. | X | X | | | X | 5 | Law (time). | | 1 |
| Kentucky | | State board of education. | X | | | | | | | | | | | | 4 | State law. | | |
| Louisiana | | State board of education. | | X | | | | | | | | | | | Indefinite | State department. | ¼ new adoptions each year. Availability of textbooks. | 0 |
| Maine | X | | | | | | | | | | | | | | | | | 76 |

| State | | Authority | | Years | Authority | Number |
|---|---|---|---|---|---|---|
| Michigan | X | | | | | |
| Minnesota | X | | | | | |
| Mississippi | | State textbook purchasing board. | | | State textbook purchasing board. | 1 |
| Missouri | X | | | | | 1 |
| Montana | X | | | | | |
| Nebraska | X | | | | | |
| Nevada | | State board. | | 2 | State board of education. | 1 |
| New Hampshire | X | | | | Time. | 4 |
| New Jersey | X | | | | | 4 |
| New Mexico | | State board of education. | | 6 | Law. | M |
| New York | X | | | | | |
| North Carolina | | State board (basal texts). | | 5 or 7 | State board of education. | 2 |
| North Dakota | | Department of public instruction. | | | Law. | 1 |
| Ohio | X | | | | | 2 |
| Oklahoma | | State textbook committee. | | 4–6 | State textbook committee. | 9 |
| Oregon | | Appointed by Governor. | | 6 | Legislature. | 78 |
| Pennsylvania | X | | | | | 28 |
| Rhode Island | X | | | | | 0 |
| South Carolina | | State board of education. | | 4 | State board of education. | 46 |
| South Dakota | X | County textbook committee. | | | Obsoleteness of material. | |
| Tennessee | | State textbook commission. | | 3–5 | State textbook commission. | 158 |
| Texas | X | State board of education. | | 6 | Law, time. | 1 |
| Utah | | State law. | | 4 | State law. | 1 |
| Vermont | X | | | | | |
| Virginia | X | | | 6 | General assembly. | |
| Washington | X | | | | Time. | 56 |
| West Virginia | | State board of education. | | 4 | State law mandates. | 4 |
| Wisconsin | X | Forbidden by constitution of State. | | | | 1 |
| Wyoming | X | | | | | |
| Alaska | | Statutory. | | 4 | Textbook commission. | 1 |

—Reprinted from *Curriculum Responsibilities of State Departments of Education,* a publication of the U.S. Department of Health, Education and Welfare, U.S. Government Printing Office, Washington, 1958, pp. 22–23.

# ABOUT THE AUTHOR

ARTHER S. TRACE, JR., was born in Denver, Colorado, in 1922, and served in the Armed Forces in the United States and in Europe before being graduated from the University of Denver. He holds an MA from Columbia University and a Ph.D. from Stanford University. He has taught English at the University of Nebraska, Stanford University, and Purdue University. Now an associate professor of English, he teaches Renaissance literature and literary criticism at John Carroll University in Cleveland, Ohio. Mr. Trace is also a member of the faculty of the new Institute for Soviet and East European Studies at John Carroll University. He is the co-author of a freshman English text, *Preparatory Reading for Writing,* and has written a number of articles on education.